200 *Fast*
vegetarian recipes

KT-569-426

hamlyn | **all colour cookbook**

200 *Fast*

vegetarian recipes

An Hachette UK Company

www.hachette.co.uk

First published in Great Britain in 2015 by Hamlyn
a division of Octopus Publishing Group Ltd,
Carmelite House, 50 Victoria Embankment,
London EC4Y 0DZ
www.octopusbooks.co.uk

Copyright © Octopus Publishing Group Ltd 2015

Some of the recipes in this book have previously appeared
in other titles published by Hamlyn.

All rights reserved. No part of this work may be reproduced
or utilized in any form or by any means, electronic or
mechanical, including photocopying, recording or by any
information storage and retrieval system, without the prior
written permission of the publisher.

ISBN 13: 978-0-600-62904-7

A CIP catalogue record for this book is available
from the British Library.

Printed and bound in China.

4 5 6 7 8 9 10

Both metric and imperial measurements have been given
in all recipes. Use one set of measurements only, and not a
mixture of both.

Standard level spoon measurements are used in all recipes.
1 tablespoon = 15 ml spoon
1 teaspoon = 5 ml spoon

Ovens should be preheated to the specified temperature
– if using a fan-assisted oven, follow the manufacturer's
instructions for adjusting the time and temperature.

Fresh herbs should be used unless otherwise stated.

Eggs should be medium unless otherwise stated. The
Department of Health advises that eggs should not be
consumed raw. This book contains dishes made with raw
or lightly cooked eggs. It is prudent for more vulnerable
people such as pregnant and nursing mothers, invalids, the
elderly, babies and young children to avoid uncooked or
lightly cooked dishes made with eggs. Once prepared these
dishes should be kept refrigerated and used promptly.

This book includes dishes made with nuts and nut
derivatives. It is advisable for customers with known allergic
reactions to nuts and nut derivatives and those who may be
potentially vulnerable to these allergies, such as pregnant
and nursing mothers, invalids, the elderly, babies and
children, to avoid dishes made with nuts and nut oils. It is
also prudent to check the labels of pre-prepared ingredients
for the possible inclusion of nut derivatives.

contents

introduction

This book offers a new and flexible approach to meal-planning for busy cooks and lets you choose the recipe option that best fits the time you have available. Inside you will find 200 dishes that will inspire you and motivate you to get cooking every day of the year.

All the recipes take a maximum of 30 minutes to cook. Some take as little as 20 minutes and, amazingly, many take only 10 minutes.

On every page you'll find a main recipe plus a short-cut version or a fancier variation if you have a bit more time to spare. Whatever you go for, you'll find a huge range of super-quick recipes to get you through the week.

vegetarian recipes

A diet rich in fresh vegetables, pulses and wholegrains is well documented to be a healthy one. Armed with the knowledge that a diet high in meat protein can be detrimental to health, and with such an abundance of wonderful, seasonal vegetables widely available, it's not difficult to understand why many people choose to follow a vegetarian or 'flexitarian' diet.

The key to a well-balanced vegetarian diet is simple: eat plenty of wholegrains (brown rice, barley, corn, oats, millet and buckwheat are all good options), foods which are made from wholegrains (such as wholemeal breads, pastas and cereals), protein-rich pulses, lentils, nuts and eggs, and an abundance of fresh fruit and vegetables. Dairy products (such as butter, cheese, cream, milk and yoghurt) or non-dairy alternatives should form a smaller part of the diet and caffeinated drinks, alcohol and sugary treats should be enjoyed in moderation.

Complex carbohydrates are essential for a good diet and vital for energy. The presence of dietary fibre allows the energy from the natural sugars they contain to be released slowly, as opposed to refined sugars, which are released into the body quickly and can leave energy levels depleted. Foods rich in complex carbohydrates include those made using the whole of the grain, such as wholemeal bread and wholewheat pasta, as well as brown rice, barley, corn, buckwheat, dried beans and bananas.

A healthy vegetarian diet will be high in fibre, which is vital for moving the food in the bowel, helping to prevent intestinal problems and reducing the risk of bowel cancer. Foods rich in fibre can help to lower blood cholesterol, therefore it is advisable to include high-fibre foods, such as beans and peas, brassica family vegetables (including cabbage, broccoli and Brussels sprouts), oats and wholegrain wheat, in most of your meals.

Protein is essential for tissue repair and cell growth and reproduction, especially for growing children and pregnant women. However, we do not need large amounts of protein in our diet and it is perfectly possible to consume the recommended amounts of protein from just non-animal foods. Good sources of vegetarian protein include nuts and seeds, pulses, soya products, peas, beans, chickpeas and lentils.

techniques and tips

Using condiments, seasonings, herbs and spices can liven up your dining experience enormously, giving you an opportunity to cook and eat a glorious palette of flavours, colours and textures. Stock up your store cupboard before you begin to travel through the varied and wonderful world of vegetarian cookery. Most supermarkets will sell everything you'll need, but also try ethnic stores and greengrocers to source more unusual ingredients and produce.

A well-equipped kitchen will really help you to save time when preparing your vegetarian meals. A couple of good saucepans of different sizes, a frying pan and a wok are all essentials, and you will find lots of uses for a good-quality pestle and mortar. A salad spinner speeds-up salad washing, and accurate kitchen scales will help to ensure successful results every time. A food processor is a must for quick and easy blending and processing.

store cupboard staples

It's a good idea to have a variety of dried pasta shapes to hand – linguini, spaghetti, pappardelle, fusilli, penne and orzo should cover most recipes.

Rice (basmati, brown, jasmine, risotto and paella), bulgar wheat, couscous, polenta and quinoa are great staples that can be used in a variety of ways to produce wonderful, quick meals. Plain flour is a must for making sauce bases and crumble toppings. Gram flour is great for a spiced batter base to make a variety of crispy vegetable fritters.

Quick-cooking pulses that don't require long soaking – Puy lentils, split red lentils and yellow split peas –are essential for creating delicious vegetarian dishes, and canned pulses and beans are handy for instant, last-minute meals. A good supply of kidney beans, chickpeas, black-eyed beans, cannellini beans and butter beans will also be really useful.

Healthy, wholesome and delicious, nuts and seeds will perk-up many dishes from salads to stir-fries. Sunflower seeds, sesame seeds, cashew nuts, almonds, pistachio and walnuts make nutritious additions to vegetarian meals.

Packed with flavour and colour, canned tomatoes and passatta have a multitude of uses and are a terrific stand-by for making quick sauces, curries and stews.

Good-quality olive oil, sunflower and vegetable oils and toasted sesame seed oil are great for stir-frying and general-purpose cooking. Red wine, white wine, balsamic, cider and rice wine vinegars are a must for creating quick salad dressings and sauces.

flavourings

You cannot have enough of a variety of dried herbs and spices in your store cupboard to experiment with flavours. The list is endless, but always remember to buy them in small quantities and use within three months for maximum flavour. A good stock of dried herbs (basil, thyme, oregano, tarragon, rosemary and parsley are a good starting point), whole spices (cumin seeds, coriander seeds, black mustard seeds, cloves, cardamom pods and cinnamon sticks) and ground spices (cumin, cinnamon, coriander, chilli powder, paprika and turmeric) will really add depth to your dishes. Sea salt and fresh black peppercorns are also a must.

Stock up on a selection of sauces and condiments to add instant flavour to your dishes. Soy sauce, sweet chilli sauce, Tabasco sauce and Worcestershire sauce are staples you will use time and time again. Honey and maple syrup are good sweeteners to keep at hand for both sweet and savoury recipes.

fresh food

Keeping your fridge well stocked will enable you to create healthy and tasty vegetarian meals in minutes. The key is to buy fresh produce regularly, and to only buy what you know you will use to minimize wastage. Fresh pasta, tofu, cheese, butter, milk, cream and eggs are always great to have in the fridge. You'll also find lemons, limes, red chillies, fresh ginger, spring onions and fresh herbs are excellent additions to speedy meals.

Buy fruit and vegetables that are in season and, if possible, locally grown. The goodness and flavour will be far superior to those that have been grown out of season or have travelled many miles to reach the supermarket shelves. Garlic, onions, potatoes, shallots, carrots and other root vegetables and most varieties of fruit will keep well for a few days in the pantry.

snacks & light bites

quick quesadillas

Serves **4**

Total cooking time **10 minutes**

200 g (7 oz) **refried beans**

8 **soft flour tortillas**

25 g (1 oz) **jalapeño pepper slices**, drained and chopped

1 **large tomato**, deseeded and diced

150 g (5 oz) **Cheddar cheese**, grated

2 **spring onions**, sliced

1 tablespoon finely chopped **fresh coriander** (optional)

100 ml (3½ fl oz) **soured cream,** to serve (optional)

Spread the refried beans over 4 of the tortillas. Top with the jalapeño slices, diced tomato, grated cheese, spring onions and chopped coriander, if using. Cover each one with another tortilla to make 4 quesadillas.

Toast the quesadillas, one at a time, in a large ridged griddle pan set over a medium-high heat for about 30–60 seconds on each side, until lightly browned and the cheese inside has melted.

Cut the quesadillas into quarters and serve immediately with soured cream, if using.

For spicy bean burritos, spread the refried beans over all 8 tortillas, then top with the jalapeño slices, 2 large, diced tomatoes, 1 cored, deseeded and chopped red pepper and the sliced spring onion. Tuck in the ends and roll each tortilla tightly, then place in a snug-fitting ovenproof dish. Pour a 300 g (10 oz) jar hot Mexican salsa over the tortillas, then dot with small spoonfuls of soured cream and sprinkle with the cheese. Cook in a preheated oven, 220°C (425°F), Gas Mark 7, for 20–25 minutes until hot and bubbling. Serve hot with shredded iceberg lettuce and the chopped coriander, if using. **Total cooking time 30 minutes.**

stuffed courgettes

Serves **4**
Total cooking time **30 minutes**

4 **courgettes**
175 g (6 oz) **plum tomatoes**,
  chopped
210 g (7 oz) **mozzarella
  cheese**, grated
2 tablespoons shredded **basil
  leaves**
25 g (1 oz) **Italian-style hard
  cheese**, grated
salt and **pepper**

Slice the courgettes in half horizontally and then scoop out the middle of each one, reserving the flesh.

Place the courgette halves in a roasting tin, cut side up, and bake in a preheated oven, 200°C (400°F), Gas Mark 6, for 10 minutes.

Meanwhile, chop the reserved courgette flesh and mix it in a bowl with the chopped tomatoes, grated mozzarella and basil. Season to taste.

Remove the courgette halves from the oven and spoon the filling into each one.

Sprinkle with the grated Italian-style hard cheese and return to the oven to bake for 15 minutes, until golden.

For griddled courgettes with mozzarella, use a vegetable peeler to thinly slice 4 courgettes lengthways. Toss the courgettes in 2 tablespoons olive oil and then cook them on a preheated hot griddle pan for 2–3 minutes on both sides, until griddle marks start to show. Served topped with 210 g (7 oz) torn mozzarella cheese and 6–8 torn basil leaves. Drizzle with a little olive oil, a squeeze of lemon juice and a grinding of pepper. **Total cooking time 20 minutes.**

asparagus frittata

Serves **4**
Total cooking time **30 minutes**

400 g (13 oz) **asparagus**
2 tablespoons **olive oil**
6 **large eggs**
50 g (2 oz) **Italian-style hard cheese**, grated
1 tablespoon chopped **oregano**
salt and **pepper**

Break the woody ends off the asparagus and discard. Toss the spears in 1 tablespoon of the olive oil.

Heat a griddle pan until hot and cook the asparagus for 4–5 minutes, until starting to look a little charred. Cut the asparagus spears into thirds.

Beat the eggs in a large bowl with the grated Italian-style hard cheese, oregano and some salt and pepper. Add the asparagus.

Heat the remaining oil in a flameproof, nonstick frying pan. Pour the mixture into the pan and cook for 8–10 minutes over a low heat, tipping the pan from time to time to allow the runny egg to reach the edges to cook evenly.

Cook for a further 4–5 minutes under a preheated hot grill, until the top is golden.

Turn the frittata out on to a board, cut into wedges and serve immediately.

For griddled asparagus, toss 450 g (14½ oz) trimmed asparagus in 2 tablespoons olive oil. Heat a griddle pan until hot and cook the asparagus for 4–5 minutes, turning once. Serve drizzled with olive oil and sprinkled with Italian-style hard cheese shavings. **Total cooking time 10 minutes.**

falafel with spicy sauce

Serves **4**
Total cooking time **15 minutes**

400 g (13 oz) **can chickpeas**,
   rinsed and drained
1 **onion**, finely diced
2 **garlic** cloves, chopped
3 tablespoons chopped
   parsley
1 teaspoon **ground coriander**
1 teaspoon **ground cumin**
2 tablespoons **plain flour**
2–3 tablespoons **vegetable
   oil**
salt and **pepper**
½ **iceburg lettuce**, shredded,
   to serve

Spicy sauce
100 g (3½ oz) **tomato purée**
½ –1 teaspoon **harissa paste**,
   to taste
2 **garlic cloves**, crushed
1 teaspoon **lemon juice**
50 ml (2 fl oz) **water**
1 tablespoon chopped **parsley**

To make the sauce, place all the ingredients in a small saucepan and simmer for 10 minutes.

Meanwhile, place all the falafel ingredients except the oil in a large bowl and mash together with a fork. Season to taste. Alternatively, place the ingredients in a food processor and blitz until smooth. Using wet hands, shape the mixture into small balls and flatten slightly.

Heat the vegetable oil in a frying pan and cook the falafel for 5–7 minutes, turning once, until goldenall over.

Serve on the lettuce with the spicy sauce.

For falafel & tabbouleh salad, make the falafel as above. Meanwhile, place 250 g (8 oz) couscous in a heatproof bowl and just cover with boiling water. Leave to stand for 10 minutes. Fluff up the couscous with a fork, then stir in 2 tablespoons each of chopped mint, parsley and chives, 3 diced tomatoes and ½ diced cucumber. Serve with the falafel and dollops of ready-made hummus. **Total cooking time 20 minutes.**

aubergine melts

Serves **4**
Total cooking time **30 minutes**

2 **aubergines**, halved
   lengthways
4 tablespoons **olive oil**
4 **tomatoes**, sliced
200 g (7 oz) **mozzarella**
   cheese, sliced
a small handful of **basil leaves**
2 tablespoons **toasted pine**
   nuts
pepper
crisp **green salad**, to serve

Place the aubergine halves on a baking sheet, drizzle with the olive oil and bake in a preheated oven, 200°C (400°F), Gas Mark 6 for 20 minutes until softened.

Remove the aubergine from the oven, arrange the slices of tomato and mozzarella on top and bake for a further 5 minutes, until the cheese has melted.

Scatter with basil leaves and pine nuts, season with pepper and serve with a crisp green salad.

For aubergine & goats' cheese pasta, cook 400 g (13 oz) pasta shapes of your choice in a saucepan of boiling water according to the pack instructions, until 'al dente'. Meanwhile, heat 1 tablespoon olive oil in a frying pan and fry 1 chopped onion and 2 sliced garlic cloves for 3–4 minutes. Add 1 chopped aubergine and cook for a further 4–5 minutes. Pour in a 400 g (13 oz) can chopped tomatoes and simmer for 3–4 minutes. Drain the pasta and stir into the sauce with 100 g (3½ oz) crumbled goats' cheese and a small handful of torn basil leaves and mix well. **Total cooking time 20 minutes.**

sweetcorn fritters with chilli salsa

Serves **4**

Total cooking time **20 minutes**

275 g (9 oz) **can sweetcorn**
65 g (2½ oz) **plain flour**
1 teaspoon **baking powder**
1 **egg**, beaten
½ **red pepper**, cored,
   deseeded and finely
   chopped
1 small **red chilli**, deseeded
   and finely chopped
6 tablespoons chopped **fresh
coriander**
2 tablespoons **vegetable oil**
pepper

Salsa
1 tablespoon **olive oil**
2 **tomatoes**, finely chopped
½ small **red chilli**, finely
   chopped
1 tablespoon **soft light brown
sugar**
2 tablespoons chopped **fresh
coriander**

Drain the sweetcorn and place half the kernels in a food processor and whizz until almost smooth. Transfer to a bowl and stir in the remaining, whole sweetcorn. Sift in the flour and baking powder and mix together. Mix in the egg, red pepper, chilli and coriander and season with plenty of pepper.

Heat the oil in a large, heavy-based non-stick frying pan over a medium-high heat and drop in 4 spoonfuls of the mixture. Cook for about 1 minute on each side until browned. Remove with a fish slice, drain on kitchen paper and keep warm. Cook the remaining mixture in the same way (to make 8 fritters in total).

Meanwhile, mix together all the ingredients for the salsa, season with pepper and place in a serving bowl.

Serve the fritters warm with the salsa on the side.

For sweetcorn pancakes, make up a 150 g (5 oz) packet pancake batter mix according to the pack instructions and mix in 8 tablespoons drained canned sweetcorn and 3 tablespoons chopped fresh coriander. Season well. Heat a little vegetable oil in a frying pan over a medium-high heat, pour in a quarter of the mixture and cook for 1 minute, then turn and cook for a few seconds on the other side. Cook the remaining mixture in the same way. Fill the pancakes with shop-bought tomato salsa and a few rocket leaves, if liked. **Total cooking time 10 minutes.**

tostados with avocado & tomato

Serves **4**
Total cooking time **10 minutes**

4 **corn tortillas**
1 tablespoon **vegetable oil**
2 **avocados**, peeled and
    stoned
50 ml (2 fl oz) **crème fraîche**
2–3 tablespoons **lime juice**
4 **tomatoes**, chopped
1 tablespoon finely chopped
    red onion
1 tablespoon **extra virgin
    olive oil**
handful of **fresh coriander**,
    chopped, plus extra to serve
    (optional)
salt and **pepper**

Use a 5 cm (2 inch) biscuit cutter to stamp out rounds
from the tortillas; alternatively, cut them into wedges.
Brush them with vegetable oil, place on a baking sheet
under a preheated hot grill and cook for 1 minute on
each side until crisp. Leave to cool.

Meanwhile, place the avocado flesh and crème fraîche
in a food processor and blend until smooth. Stir in
1 tablespoon of lime juice and season to taste. Stir
together the tomatoes, onion and olive oil, add lime
juice to taste, season and stir through the coriander.

Spoon a little of the avocado mixture on to each tortilla
round, scatter over the tomato salsa and top with more
coriander, if liked.

For tomato & tortilla soup, heat 1 tablespoon olive
oil in a saucepan, add 1 finely chopped onion and cook
for 5 minutes until softened. Add 3 finely chopped
garlic cloves and stir around the pan. Add 2 teaspoons
chipotle purée, 400 g (13 oz) can chopped tomatoes,
1 teaspoon brown sugar and a pinch of dried oregano.
Pour over 1 litre (1¾ pints) vegetable stock, bring to
the boil, reduce the heat and simmer for 10 minutes.
Use a stick blender to whizz together until smooth,
then season to taste. Cut 2 corn tortillas into thin strips.
Heat a large frying pan, add 1 tablespoon vegetable oil
and cook the tortillas for 1–2 minutes until golden and
crisp. Spoon the soup into bowls. Top with the chopped
flesh of 1 avocado, 50 g (2 oz) crumbled feta, the crisp
tortillas and a handful of chopped fresh coriander. **Total
cooking time 30 minutes.**

mozzarella & spinach pancakes

Serves **4**
Total cooking time **20 minutes**

125 g (4 oz) **plain flour**
a pinch of **salt**
2 **eggs**
200 ml (7 fl oz) **milk** mixed
   with 75 ml (3 fl oz) **water**
50 g (2 oz) **butter**, melted
200 g (7 oz) **baby spinach
   leaves**
4 **tomatoes**, sliced
400 g (13 oz) **mozzarella
   cheese**, sliced
2 tablespoons grated **Italian-
   style hard cheese**

Sift the flour and salt into a large bowl. Make a well in the centre and break the eggs into it. Whisk the eggs into the flour and then gradually add a small amount of the milk and water, still whisking.

Whisk half the melted butter into the pancake batter and use the remainder to grease a frying pan. Rub the pan with kitchen paper to take off any excess.

Pour about 2 tablespoons of the batter into the pan and swirl around to completely coat the base. After 1 minute check that the pancake is cooked underneath and then flip it over to cook the other side for just a few more seconds.

Sprinkle half the pancake with some spinach leaves, sliced tomatoes and sliced mozzarella. Fold the other half of the pancake over the filled side and press lightly. Transfer the filled pancake to an ovenproof dish and keep warm.

Repeat with the remaining ingredients. Sprinkle the pancakes with the grated Italian-style hard cheese and briefly cook under a preheated hot grill until the pancakes are golden. Serve immediately.

For mozzarella & spinach salad, layer 100 g (3½ oz) spinach leaves with 400 g (13 oz) sliced mozzarella cheese, 2 thinly sliced beefsteak tomatoes and 10–12 basil leaves on a large platter. Sprinkle with 2 teaspoons chopped oregano and 2 tablespoons toasted pine nuts and drizzle with 3 tablespoons extra virgin olive oil and 1 tablespoon balsamic vinegar. **Total cooking time 10 minutes.**

bocconcini with fresh pesto aïoli

Serves **4**
Total cooking time **20 minutes**

100 g (3½ oz) **fresh white breadcrumbs**
zest of 1 **lemon**, finely grated
generous pinch of **chilli flakes**
2 tablespoons **thyme leaves**
50 g (2 oz) **plain flour**
2 large **eggs**, beaten
300 g (10 oz) **bocconcini (baby mozzarella balls)**, drained
vegetable oil, for deep-frying
salt and **pepper**

Fresh pesto aïoli
6 tablespoons **fresh ready-made green pesto**
200 g (7 oz) **fresh mayonnaise**
2 **garlic cloves**, crushed

Make the pesto aïoli by mixing together all the ingredients. Set aside.

Mix together the breadcrumbs, lemon zest, a few chilli flakes, a sprinkling of the thyme and some seasoning in a medium bowl. Place the flour in a second bowl and the eggs in a third.

Pat the mozzarella balls dry with kitchen paper. Roll the balls first in flour, then dip in the egg, then roll in the breadcrumb mixture. Repeat in the egg and breadcrumbs to create a double layer.

Half fill a saucepan or deep-fat fryer with vegetable oil. Just before serving, heat over a high heat to 180°C (350°F) or until a cube of bread sizzles and turns golden in 10–15 seconds. Using a spider strainer or slotted spoon, lower batches of the crumbed mozzarella into the hot oil and fry for 3–4 minutes until golden brown. Remove and drain on kitchen paper.

Serve immediately with the fresh pesto aïoli.

For tomato, bocconcini & basil tricolore salad, slice 4 tomatoes and place in a wide salad bowl with a small handful basil leaves and 300 g (10 oz) bocconcini. Drizzle over 4 tablespoons extra virgin olive oil and squeeze over the juice of 1 lemon. Season well and serve with ciabatta bread. **Total cooking time 10 minutes.**

eggs florentine

Serves **4**

Total cooking time **10 minutes**

15 g (½ oz) **butter**, plus extra
for buttering the muffins
200 g (7 oz) **spinach leaves**
4 **muffins**, split in half
4 **eggs**
3 tablespoons chopped
parsley
200 ml (7 fl oz) **ready-made
hollandaise sauce**
salt and **pepper**

Half-fill a small saucepan with water and bring to the
boil. Meanwhile, melt the butter in a large saucepan, add
the spinach and cook over a medium heat, stirring, for
1–2 minutes until wilted. Season with salt and pepper.

Toast the muffins, cut-side up, under a preheated
medium grill until lightly browned. Meanwhile, poach
the eggs, 2 at a time, in the boiling water and cook for
1–2 minutes until the whites are firm and the yolks soft.

Butter the warm muffins, then divide the spinach
between them and top with an egg. Mix the parsley
into the hollandaise and spoon over the eggs. Top
with ground black pepper and serve immediately.

For eggs Florentine with leek & cheese sauce, melt
25 g (1 oz) butter in a saucepan and cook 2 finely sliced
leeks over a medium heat, stirring, for 3–4 minutes
until soft and beginning to brown. Stir in 25 g (1 oz)
plain flour, then remove from the heat and add 400 ml
(14 fl oz) milk, a little at a time, blending well between
each addition. Add 1 teaspoon prepared English mustard
and stir well, then return to the heat and bring to the boil,
stirring constantly, until thickened. Stir in 2 tablespoons
freshly grated Italian-style hard cheese. Cook and
prepare the spinach, eggs and muffins as above, then
assemble with the leek and cheese sauce instead of the
parsley hollandaise, serving with extra grated cheese, if
liked. **Total cooking time 20 minutes.**

spring onion rostis with spicy salsa

Serves **4**

Total cooking time **30 minutes**

875 g (1¾ lb) boiled **potatoes (King Edward or Maris Piper)**

6 **spring onions**, finely chopped

2 **garlic cloves**, very finely chopped

1 large **egg**, lightly beaten

4 tablespoons **sunflower oil**

lime wedges, to serve

Salsa

2 **plum tomatoes**, deseeded and roughly chopped

1 **red chilli**, deseeded and finely chopped

1 small **red onion**, halved and very thinly sliced

4 tablespoons finely chopped **fresh coriander**

2 **avocados**, peeled, stoned and roughly sliced

juice of 2 **limes**

1 tablespoon **avocado oil**

salt and **pepper**

Make the salsa by mixing all the ingredients together in a bowl. Season well and set aside until ready to serve.

Peel and coarsely grate the potatoes. Add the spring onions, garlic and egg and use your fingers to combine the mixture evenly.

Heat a large, nonstick frying pan over a high heat and add half of the oil.

Working in batches, divide the potato mixture into 8 portions. Spoon 4 of the portions into the oil and pat down to form rostis about 8–10 cm (3–4 in) in diameter. Cook for 3–4 minutes on each side and then carefully transfer to a large nonstick baking sheet. Repeat with the remaining oil and potato mixture to make 8 rostis.

Serve the rostis accompanied by the salsa and the lime wedges.

For spring onion & potato broth, place 12 sliced spring onions, 400 g (13 oz) cooked, cubed potatoes, 2 crushed garlic cloves, 4 tablespoons chopped fresh coriander leaves, 600 ml (1 pint) hot vegetable stock and 500 ml (17 fl oz) milk in a saucepan. Bring to the boil and cook for 5–6 minutes or until piping hot. Season and serve immediately. **Total cooking time 10 minutes**.

walnut, gorgonzola & pear boats

Serves **4**
Total cooking time **10 minutes**

1 **ripe pear**, cored and finely
   chopped
2 tablespoons **crème fraîche**
65 g (2½ oz) **Gorgonzola**
   cheese, crumbled
20 **red** or **green Belgian**
   chicory leaves (or a mixture
   of both)
25 g (1 oz) **walnuts**, toasted
   and roughly chopped
olive oil, to drizzle

Mix together the pear, crème fraîche and Gorgonzola
in a small bowl.

Arrange the chicory leaves on a serving platter and
spoon a little of the pear mixture on to the base of
each leaf.

Sprinkle the chopped nuts over the top of the filling,
drizzle with a little olive oil, and serve.

For baked chicory & gorgonzola, trim any coarse or
bruised outer leaves from 8 large heads red chicory.
Place in a baking dish into which they will fit snugly in
a single layer. Drizzle over 6 tablespoons olive oil and
season to taste. Scatter over 100 g (3½ oz) crumbled
Gorgonzola cheese and the juice of 1 lemon. Bake
in a preheated oven, 180°C (350°F), Gas Mark 4, for
20 minutes. Serve straight from the baking dish with
the juices and scatter over 4 tablespoons chopped
toasted walnuts before serving. **Total cooking time
30 minutes.**

borlotti bean & pepper bruschetta

Serves **4**
Total cooking time **20 minutes**

1 **large baguette**, cut into
   8 slices
3 tablespoons **olive oil**
1 **garlic clove**
400 g (13 oz) **can borlotti**
  beans, rinsed and drained
3 **spring onions**, sliced
100 g (3½ oz) **roasted red**
  peppers from a jar, drained
  and finely sliced
6 **basil leaves**, thinly shredded
salt and **pepper**

Place the slices of baguette on a baking sheet and drizzle with 2 tablespoons of the olive oil. Cook under a preheated hot grill for 2–3 minutes on each side, until toasted and golden.

Rub each slice of toast with the garlic clove.

Place the drained borlotti beans and spring onions in a bowl and lightly crush together with a fork.

Stir in the red pepper, basil, remaining olive oil and some salt and pepper.

Spoon the bean mixture on to the toasted baguette slices and serve immediately.

For quick bean salad, in a large serving bowl, mix together a 400 g (13 oz) can borlotti beans, rinsed and drained, 3 sliced spring onions, 100 g (3½ oz) drained and chopped roasted red peppers from a jar, 3 chopped tomatoes, 4–5 shredded basil leaves, 2 tablespoons olive oil and 1 tablespoon balsamic vinegar. **Total cooking time 10 minutes.**

red pepper dip with herby pittas

Serves **4**
Total cooking time **20 minutes**

5 tablespoons **olive oil**
1 **shallot**, finely chopped
100 g (3½ oz) **walnut halves**
200 g (7 oz) **ready-roasted
red peppers** from a jar
1 **garlic clove**, crushed
1 teaspoon **ground cumin**
1 tablespoon **pomegranate
molasses**
4 **pitta breads**
handful of chopped **parsley**
handful of chopped **mint**
coarse sea salt

Heat 1 tablespoon of the oil in a frying pan, add the shallot and cook for 3 minutes until softened. Leave to cool.

Toast the walnut halves in a dry frying pan for 3 minutes until lightly browned and leave to cool. Put the walnuts in a blender with the shallot, peppers, garlic, cumin, pomegranate molasses and 2 tablespoons of the oil and whizz together until smooth. Season to taste.

Meanwhile, split the pittas open horizontally and cut each half into wedges. Mix together the remaining oil with the herbs and brush over the wedges. Place on a baking sheet, sprinkle with coarse sea salt and bake in a preheated oven, 190°C (375°F), Gas Mark 5, for 5–7 minutes or until golden and crisp. Serve alongside the red pepper dip.

For herb & roasted pepper salad, lightly toast 25 g (1 oz) walnut halves in a dry frying pan. Whisk 1 tablespoon sherry vinegar with 3 tablespoons olive oil. Toss with 150 g (5 oz) mixed herb salad and 2 ready-roasted red peppers, cut into strips. Season to taste. Arrange on a plate, then scatter over the walnuts and 50 g (2 oz) crumbled soft goats' cheese. **Total cooking time 10 minutes.**

baked brie with maple syrup

Serves **4**
Total cooking time **20 minutes**

300 g (10 oz) **whole baby
  Brie** or **Camembert**
25 g (1 oz) **pecans**
3 tablespoons **maple syrup**
3 tablespoons **soft dark
  brown sugar**
thyme sprigs
crusty bread, to serve

Remove any plastic packaging from the cheese and return it to its wooden box. Place on a baking sheet and cook in a preheated oven, 200°C (400°F), Gas Mark 6, for 15 minutes.

Meanwhile, toast the pecans in a small frying pan for 3–5 minutes until lightly browned, then set aside. Put the maple syrup and sugar in a small saucepan and bring to the boil. Cook for 1 minute until foamy.

Take the cheese from the oven and cut a small cross in the centre. Drizzle over the maple syrup, scatter with the pecans and thyme and serve with plenty of crusty bread.

For brie salad with maple dressing, whisk together 1 tablespoon maple syrup with 1 teaspoon mustard, 1 tablespoon white wine vinegar and 3 tablespoons olive oil. Season and toss together with 200 g (7 oz) mixed salad leaves. Arrange on plates with 25 g (1 oz) toasted pecans. Cut 125 g (4 oz) Brie into thick slices. Put the Brie on a baking sheet and cook under a hot grill for 1 minute or until starting to melt. Scatter over the salad to serve. **Total cooking time 10 minutes.**

broad bean & pea crostini

Serves **6**
Total cooking time **20 minutes**

75 ml (3 fl oz) **olive oil**
1 **lemon**
2 **garlic cloves**, peeled
300 g (10 oz) **broad beans**
300 g (10 oz) **peas**
handful of **mint leaves**
6 slices of **sourdough bread**
salt and **pepper**

To serve
2 **radishes**, thinly sliced
handful of **pea shoots**
**Italian-style hard cheese
  shavings**

Put the oil, 3 strips of lemon rind and the garlic cloves in a small pan and cook over a very low heat for 7–10 minutes. Remove from the heat and discard the lemon rind.

Cook the broad beans and peas in a pan of lightly salted boiling water for 3 minutes until just soft. Drain and rinse under cold running water to cool. Peel the broad beans and discard the shells.

Tip most of the peas and beans into a blender, add the mint and cooked garlic together with the flavoured oil and pulse to make a rough purée. Season well.

Toast the bread, halve the slices and arrange on a serving platter. Spread with the purée and scatter with the reserved peas and broad beans. Top with radishes, pea shoots and Italian-style hard cheese shavings and serve.

For pea & broad bean salad, cook 100 g (3½ oz) each of peas and broad beans in lightly salted boiling water for 3 minutes until soft, drain and cool under cold running water. Whisk 3 tablespoons olive oil with 1 tablespoon lemon juice, season and toss with 150 g (5 oz) salad leaves. Place on serving plates, scatter over the peas and beans and top with Italian-style hard cheese shavings to serve. **Total cooking time 10 minutes.**

asparagus with poached eggs

Serves **4**

Total cooking time **10 minutes**

700 g (1 lb 6 oz) **asparagus spears**

1 tablespoon **olive oil**

4 **eggs**

40 g (1¾ oz) **Italian-style hard cheese**

Snap the woody ends off the asparagus spears and discard. Heat a griddle pan until very hot and sprinkle it with the oil.

Meanwhile, bring a frying pan of water to the boil for the eggs.

Place the asparagus on the griddle and cook, turning regularly, until slightly charred at the ends.

Stir the boiling water vigorously then, one at a time, drop the cracked eggs into the centre – the swirling water will help the egg white collect around the yolk and maintain the shape of the egg. Cook for 4–5 minutes then remove with a slotted spoon.

Serve the asparagus on 4 warmed plates, and top with the poached eggs.

Using a vegetable peeler, make curly shavings of Italian-style hard cheese and sprinkle on top of the asparagus.

For asparagus omelette, heat 1 tablespoon oil in a frying pan, add 6 chopped asparagus spears, 2 sliced spring onions and 3–4 sliced chestnut mushrooms and cook for 5–6 minutes. Whisk together 5 eggs and 4 tablespoons milk and pour into the pan, tipping the pan and moving the egg with a spatula to ensure it all cooks. Sprinkle with 25 g (1 oz) grated Italian-style hard cheese, then place under a preheated hot grill for 1–2 minutes, until golden. Cut into quarters and serve with a green salad and new potatoes. **Total cooking time 20 minutes.**

chickpea & spinach omelette

Serves **4**

Total cooking time **20 minutes**

2 tablespoons **olive oil**

1 **large onion**, sliced

1 **red pepper**, cored,
   deseeded and sliced

½ teaspoon **hot smoked** or
   sweet paprika

400 g (13 oz) **can chickpeas**,
   drained and rinsed

100 g (3½ oz) **spinach
   leaves**, rinsed and
   roughly sliced

5 **eggs**, lightly beaten

75 g (3 oz) **pitted green
   olives**, roughly chopped

150 g (5 oz) **Cheddar cheese**,
   grated

salt and **pepper**

Heat the olive oil in a large nonstick frying pan. Add the onion and pepper and cook gently for 7–8 minutes, until soft and golden. Stir in the paprika and chickpeas, and cook for 1 minute, stirring frequently. Add the spinach leaves and cook until just wilted.

Pour the beaten eggs into the pan and stir to combine. Cook gently, without stirring, for 4–5 minutes, until almost set.

Sprinkle with the olives and grated Cheddar, then slide under a hot grill, keeping the handle away from the heat. Grill for 4–5 minutes, until golden and set. Slice into wedges and serve immediately.

For chickpea & spinach salad with poached eggs, heat 2 tablespoons olive oil in a large frying pan. Add 1 sliced onion and 1 deseeded and sliced red pepper, and cook gently for 7–8 minutes. Stir in ½ teaspoon hot smoked or sweet paprika and 400 g (13 oz) can chickpeas, drained and rinsed, and cook for 1 minute, stirring frequently. Meanwhile, poach 4 eggs in a large pan of gently simmering water. Toss the chickpea mixture briefly with 200 g (7 oz) baby spinach leaves and heap on to 4 serving plates. Top each salad with a poached egg and serve immediately. **Total cooking time 10 minutes.**

bean burgers with garlicky yogurt

Serves **4**
Total cooking time **30 minutes**

3 tablespoons **vegetable oil**
1 **onion**, finely chopped
1 **garlic clove**, chopped
400 g (13 oz) **can kidney
   beans**, drained and rinsed
400 g (13 oz) **can black-eyed
   beans**, drained and rinsed
1 tablespoon **tomato purée**
1 teaspoon **paprika** (optional)
4 tablespoons finely chopped
   flat leaf parsley
1 small **egg**, lightly beaten
100 g (3½ oz) **fresh white
   breadcrumbs**
250 ml (8 fl oz) **natural yogurt**
1 small **garlic clove**, crushed
2 teaspoons **lemon juice**
salt and **pepper**
4 **soft flour tortillas**, warmed,
   to serve
lettuce leaves, to garnish

Heat 2 tablespoons of the oil in a small frying pan
and cook the onion gently for 6–7 minutes. Add the
chopped garlic and cook for a further 2–3 minutes,
until really soft and golden.

Meanwhile, place both lots of beans in the large bowl
of a food processor with the tomato purée, paprika,
if using, and half the parsley. Pulse until the mixture
becomes a coarse paste. Tip into a bowl and add the
egg, breadcrumbs and cooked onion mixture. Season
with salt and pepper, then mix well and shape into
4 large burgers.

Heat the remaining oil in a large nonstick frying pan
and fry the burgers gently for 8–10 minutes, turning
once, until crisp and golden.

Meanwhile, mix the yogurt with the crushed garlic,
the remaining parsley and the lemon juice. Season
with salt and pepper and set aside.

Serve the burgers with warmed tortillas and the yogurt
and garnish with lettuce leaves.

For mixed bean hummus, place a 400 g (13 oz)
can mixed beans, rinsed and drained, in a food
processor with 1 tablespoon tomato purée, 1 teaspoon
paprika, 4 tablespoons finely chopped flat leaf parsley,
1 small crushed garlic clove and 2 teaspoons lemon
juice, and blend to a paste. Add enough yogurt to give
a smooth, creamy consistency, then season to taste
and serve with a selection of raw vegetables for
dipping. **Total cooking time 10 minutes.**

feta-stuffed peppers

Serves **4**
Total cooking time **20 minutes**

1 tablespoon **olive oil**
4 **long peppers**
2 **egg yolks**
200 g (8 oz) **feta cheese**,
    crumbled
3 tablespoons **natural yogurt**
finely grated rind of ½ **lemon**
1 teaspoon chopped **oregano**

Rub the oil over the peppers, arrange them in a grill pan and cook under a preheated hot grill for 5 minutes, turning once, until just soft. Leave to cool for a couple of minutes, then cut in half lengthways and remove the seeds.

Place the egg yolks, three-quarters of the feta, the yogurt and lemon rind in a food processor and blend until smooth. Spoon the mixture into the peppers, then crumble the remaining feta on top and sprinkle with the oregano.

Return to the grill and cook for 5–7 minutes until golden and cooked through. Leave to set for a couple of minutes before serving.

For spicy baked feta with peppers, lightly grease 4 large sheets of foil. Divide 1 thinly sliced red onion between the sheets and top with 2 chopped ready-roasted peppers and a handful of halved cherry tomatoes. Place a 100 g (3½ oz) chunk of feta cheese on top of each portion and divide a handful of chopped oregano and 1 sliced red chilli between them. Drizzle over a little olive oil, then fold up the foil to make airtight parcels. Place on a baking sheet and cook in a preheated oven, 200°C (400°F), Gas Mark 6, for 20 minutes. Serve with plenty of crusty bread. **Total cooking time 30 minutes.**

ciabatta toast with grilled veg

Serves **4**
Total cooking time **10 minutes**

5 tablespoons **olive oil**, plus
   extra for drizzling
½ **aubergine**, trimmed and
   thinly sliced
1 **ciabatta loaf**
4 tablespoons **green pesto**
1 **large beef tomato**, thinly
   sliced
4 slices of **mozzarella cheese**
pepper

Heat the oil in a large, heavy-based frying pan and cook the aubergine slices in batches over a high heat for 1–2 minutes on each side until browned and tender. Remove with a fish slice and keep warm.

Meanwhile, cut the ciabatta loaf in half lengthways, then each half in half again widthways. Place on the grill rack and cook under a preheated high grill, cut-side up, for 1 minute until golden.

Spread each ciabatta toastie with 1 tablespoon of the pesto. Top with the warm aubergine slices, then the tomato slices and finally the mozzarella slices. Drizzle each toastie with 1 tablespoon olive oil, then return to the grill and cook for a further 2 minutes until the mozzarella is melting and beginning to brown in places.

Season with pepper and serve warm.

For Mediterranean vegetable gratin, gently heat 4 tablespoons olive oil in a large frying pan and cook 1 sliced aubergine in batches over a high heat for 1–2 minutes on each side until browned and tender. Loosely layer in a large, shallow gratin dish with 3 sliced large beef tomatoes, 2 x 150 g (5 oz) packs mozzarella cheese, drained and thinly sliced, and 6 tablespoons green pesto, seasoning between the layers. Scatter with 3 tablespoons freshly grated Italian-style hard cheese and cook under a preheated high grill for 8–10 minutes until golden and bubbling. **Total cooking time 30 minutes.**

soups & salads

lettuce, pea & tarragon soup

Serves **4**
Total cooking time **20 minutes**

2 tablespoons **butter**
8 **spring onions**, trimmed
and sliced
750 g (1½ lb) **frozen peas**
1 tablespoon chopped
tarragon leaves
1 **romaine lettuce**, finely
shredded
1 litre (1¾ pints) **hot**
vegetable stock
2 tablespoons **double cream**
salt and **pepper**
tarragon sprigs, to garnish
(optional)

Melt the butter in a large saucepan over a medium heat. Add the spring onions and cook, stirring continuously, for 2 minutes.

Stir in the peas, half the tarragon and the lettuce. Cook for 1 minute.

Add the stock, bring to the boil, cover and simmer for 5 minutes or until tender.

Pour the soup into a blender, add the remaining tarragon and whizz until smooth. Season to taste.

Divide the soup between 4 bowls, swirl the cream into each bowl and sprinkle with black pepper. Garnish with tarragon sprigs, if liked.

For lettuce, pea, tomato & spring onion salad,
separate the leaves of 2 washed romaine lettuces and place in a large, wide salad bowl with 8 sliced spring onions, 4 sliced plum tomatoes, 500 g (1 lb) blanched peas and 12 sliced radishes. Make a dressing by whisking together the juice of 1 lemon, 6 tablespoons olive oil, 1 teaspoon Dijon mustard, 2 tablespoons finely chopped tarragon and 2 teaspoons clear honey. Season and pour over the salad ingredients. Toss to mix well and serve. **Total cooking time 10 minutes.**

roasted tomato soup

Serves **4**
Total cooking time **30 minutes**

1 kg (2 lb) **ripe tomatoes**, halved
4 **garlic cloves**, unpeeled
2 tablespoons **olive oil**
1 **onion**, chopped
1 **carrot**, chopped
1 **celery stick**, sliced
1 **red pepper**, cored, deseeded and chopped
700 ml (1 pint 3 fl oz) **hot vegetable stock**
salt and **pepper**
4 tablespoons grated **Italian-style hard cheese**, to serve

Place the tomato halves and garlic cloves in a roasting tin. Sprinkle with 1 tablespoon of the olive oil and some pepper and roast in a preheated oven, 200°C (400°F), Gas Mark 6, for 20 minutes.

After 10 minutes, heat the remaining olive oil in a saucepan and sauté the onion, carrot, celery and red pepper over a low heat for 10 minutes.

When the tomatoes are cooked, remove the garlic cloves in their skins and squeeze the garlic flesh into the pan with the sautéed vegetables.

Pour in the roast tomatoes and all the juices along with the stock. Using a hand blender, or in a food processor or blender, blend the soup until smooth. Season to taste.

Reheat if necessary, then serve sprinkled with the grated Italian-style hard cheese.

For quick tomato soup, heat 2 tablespoons olive oil in a saucepan and sauté 1 chopped onion, 1 chopped carrot, 1 chopped celery stick and 700 g (1½ lb) chopped tomatoes for 5 minutes. Pour in a 400 g (13 oz) can chopped tomatoes and 900 ml (1½ pints) hot vegetable stock. Simmer for 10 minutes, remove from the heat and add a small handful of basil leaves. Using a hand blender, or in a food processor or blender, blend the soup until smooth. Season to taste and serve with an extra drizzle of olive oil. **Total cooking time 20 minutes.**

oriental soup with egg & greens

Serves **4**
Total cooking time **30 minutes**

4 **spring onions**
100 g (3½ oz) **pak choi**,
   roughly chopped
2 tablespoons **vegetable oil**
2.5 cm (1 in) piece **fresh root
   ginger**, finely grated
2 **garlic cloves**, finely chopped
200 g (7 oz) **jasmine rice**
100 ml (3½ fl oz) **rice wine**
2 tablespoons **soy sauce**
1 teaspoon **rice wine vinegar**
1 litre (1¾ pints) **hot
   vegetable stock**
4 **eggs**
1 tablespoon **chilli oil**, for
   drizzling

Finely slice the spring onions, keeping the white and
green parts separate. Combine the green bits with
the pak choi in a bowl and set aside.

Heat the oil gently in a saucepan. When hot, add
the onion whites, ginger and garlic and stir-fry for
2–3 minutes.

Add the rice, stir, then add the wine and bubble for
a minute or so.

Add the soy sauce, vinegar and stock and simmer,
stirring occasionally, for 10–12 minutes. Then stir in
the reserved spring onions and pak choi and cook for
a further 2–3 minutes. Meanwhile, poach the eggs in
two batches.

To serve, ladle the soup into 4 shallow soup bowls and
top each one with a poached egg and drizzle over the
chilli oil.

For Oriental rice & Asian green salad, place
300 g (10 oz) blanched and roughly chopped pak
choi in a salad bowl with 6 sliced spring onions and
500 g (1 lb) cooked jasmine rice. Make a dressing by
whisking together 1 crushed garlic clove, 1 teaspoon
grated ginger, ¼ teaspoon chilli oil, 2 tablespoons
light soy sauce, the juice of 2 limes, a dash of rice
wine vinegar and 4 tablespoons vegetable oil. Season,
pour over the salad and toss to mix well before serving.
Total cooking time 10 minutes

sweet potato & red pepper soup

Serves **4**
Total cooking time **20 minutes**

2 tablespoons **vegetable oil**
1 **red onion**, chopped
1 **red pepper**, cored,
   deseeded and chopped
550 g (1 lb 2 oz) **sweet
   potatoes**, peeled and
   chopped
¼ teaspoon **ground cumin**
8 **cherry tomatoes**
1.2 litres (2 pints) **vegetable
   stock**
25 g (1 oz) **creamed coconut**,
   chopped
salt and **pepper**

To serve
natural yogurt
fresh coriander sprigs

Heat the oil in a saucepan over a medium heat, add the onion and pepper and cook for 3–4 minutes. Stir in the sweet potatoes, cumin and tomatoes, and cook for a further 2–3 minutes.

Pour in the stock, bring to the boil and simmer for 12 minutes. Stir in the creamed coconut and cook for a further 2–3 minutes. Using a hand-held blender or food-processor, blend the soup until smooth.

Season with salt and pepper and serve topped with a dollop of natural yogurt and a sprig of coriander.

For warm sweet potato wedges salad, slice 900 g (1¾ lb) sweet potatoes into wedges. In a large bowl, mix together 2 crushed garlic cloves, 4 tablespoons olive oil, 2 teaspoons chopped sage, 1 teaspoon paprika and some salt and pepper. Toss the potato in the herb and spice mixture, place in a roasting tin and roast in a preheated oven, 200°C (400°F), Gas Mark 6, for 25 minutes. Serve the potato wedges tossed with 250 g (8 oz) baby spinach leaves and 4 chopped spring onions. **Total cooking time 30 minutes.**

lentil, mustard & chickpea soup

Serves **4**

Total cooking time **20 minutes**

½ teaspoon **coconut oil** or **olive oil**
¼ teaspoon **mustard seeds**
½ teaspoon **ground cumin**
½ teaspoon **ground turmeric**
1 small **onion**, diced
1.5-cm (¾-inch) piece of **fresh root ginger**, finely chopped
1 **garlic clove**, finely chopped
100 g (3½ oz) **red split lentils**
250 g (8 oz) **canned chickpeas**, rinsed and drained
900 ml (1½ pints) **hot vegetable stock**
50 g (2 oz) **baby spinach leaves**
salt and **pepper**

Heat the oil in a saucepan and add the dry spices. When the mustard seeds start to pop, add the onion, ginger and garlic and cook until the onion softens.

Add the lentils and chickpeas and stir well to coat. Pour in the stock and bring to the boil, then reduce the heat and simmer for 14–16 minutes until the lentils are cooked.

Stir in the spinach until wilted, then season to taste. Ladle the soup into bowls and serve.

For lentil & chickpea salad with warm mustard dressing, heat 3 tablespoons olive oil in a large frying pan, add 1 deseeded and chopped red chilli, ½ teaspoon mustard seeds, 2 sliced garlic cloves and a 2.5-cm (1-inch) piece of peeled and grated root ginger, and sauté for 2 minutes. Remove from the heat and stir in 1 small sliced red onion, a 400 g (13 oz) can lentils and a 400 g (13 oz) can chickpeas, rinsed and drained, the juice of ½ lemon and 2 tablespoons chopped sun-dried tomatoes. Stir together, pour into a serving bowl and toss with 60 g (2¼ oz) rocket leaves and 150 g (5 oz) crumbled feta cheese. **Total cooking time 10 minutes.**

iced green gazpacho

Serves **4**

Total preparation time
20 minutes

2 **celery sticks** (including leaves)

1 small **green pepper**, deseeded

1 large **cucumber**, peeled

3 slices **stale white bread**, crusts removed

1 **fresh green chilli**, deseeded

4 **garlic cloves**

1 teaspoon **clear honey**

150 g (5 oz) **walnuts**, lightly toasted

200 g (7 oz) **baby spinach**

50 g (2 oz) **basil leaves**

4 tablespoons **cider vinegar**

250 ml (8 fl oz) **extra virgin olive oil**, plus extra for drizzling

6 tablespoons **natural yogurt**

475 ml (16 fl oz) **iced water**

handful of **ice cubes**

salt and **pepper**

ready-made croutons, to serve

Chop roughly the celery, pepper, cucumber, bread, chilli and garlic.

Place in a blender and add the honey, walnuts, spinach, basil, vinegar, oil, yogurt, most of the iced water and the ice cubes, and season well. Whizz the soup until smooth. Add more iced water, if needed, to achieve the desired consistency.

Taste the soup and adjust the seasoning, if necessary.

Serve in chilled bowls and garnish with croutons and a drizzle of olive oil.

For green vegetable salad, place 4 thinly sliced celery sticks, 1 sliced cucumber, 1 deseeded and thinly sliced green pepper and 100 g (3½ oz) baby spinach into a large wide bowl. Make a dressing by whisking 150 ml (¼ pint) natural yogurt in a bowl with the juice of 1 lime, 1 crushed garlic clove, 1 teaspoon clear honey and 1 finely diced green chilli. Drizzle over the salad and scatter over a small handful of ready-made croutons before serving. **Total cooking time 10 minutes.**

spicy lentil & carrot soup

Serves **4**
Total cooking time **30 minutes**

2 tablespoons **sunflower oil**
1 **garlic clove**, finely chopped
1 teaspoon grated **fresh root ginger**
1 **red chilli**, finely chopped
1 **onion**, finely chopped
1 tablespoon **sweet smoked paprika**, plus extra to garnish
700 g (1½ lb) **carrots**, peeled and finely chopped
150 g (5 oz) **red split lentils**, rinsed and drained
150 ml (¼ pint) **single cream**
1 litre (1¾ pints) **hot vegetable stock**
100 ml (3½ fl oz) **crème fraîche**
small handful of chopped **fresh coriander leaves**
salt and **pepper**

Caramelized onions
1 tablespoon **butter**
1 tablespoon **olive oil**
1 **onion**, thinly sliced

Heat the sunflower oil in a heavy-based saucepan, add the garlic, ginger, red chilli, onion and smoked paprika and cook, stirring, over a medium-high heat for 1–2 minutes. Add the carrots, lentils, cream and stock and bring to the boil, then reduce the heat to medium and simmer, uncovered, for 15–20 minutes.

Meanwhile, to make the caramelized onions, heat the butter and olive oil in a frying pan, add the onion and cook over a low heat for 12–15 minutes or until caramelized and golden brown. Drain on kitchen paper and keep warm.

Using an electric stick blender or food processor, blend the lentil mixture in the pan until smooth, then season well.

Ladle into bowls, add a dollop of crème fraiche and scatter with chopped coriander leaves and the caramelized onions. Sprinkle with a little smoked paprika before serving.

For spicy lentil & carrot salad, put 2 rinsed and drained 400 g (12 oz) cans green lentils, 2 peeled and coarsely grated carrots, 1 finely chopped red chilli, 4 sliced spring onions and a large handful of chopped fresh coriander leaves in a salad bowl. Pour 150 ml (¼ pint) shop-bought fresh French salad dressing over the salad and add 1 teaspoon sweet smoked paprika. Season, toss to mix and serve. **Total cooking time 10 minutes.**

tuscan bean & truffle soup

Serves **4**
Total cooking time **20 minutes**

2 tablespoons **olive oil**
1 **onion**, chopped
2 **garlic cloves**, sliced
400 g (13 oz) **can cannellini
 beans**, rinsed and drained
400 g (13 oz) **can butter
 beans**, rinsed and drained
400 g (13 oz) **can chopped
 tomatoes**
½ **Savoy cabbage**, shredded
½ tablespoon chopped
 rosemary
850 ml (1½ pints) **vegetable
 stock**
1 teaspoon **truffle oil**
salt and **pepper**
25 g (1 oz) grated **Italian-style
 hard cheese**, to serve

Heat the oil in a saucepan over a medium heat, add
the onion and cook for 1–2 minutes until softened.

Stir the garlic, cannellini beans and butter beans into
the onions and cook for 1 minute.

Add the tomatoes, cabbage and rosemary to the
pan, then pour in the stock and the truffle oil. Mix
together well, season and bring to the boil. Simmer
for 10–12 minutes, until the cabbage is just cooked.

Divide the soup between 4 shallow dishes and sprinkle
with the Italian-style hard cheese to serve.

For tuscan bean & truffle salad, steam 150 g (5 oz)
trimmed green beans for 2–3 minutes, then refresh
under cold running water and toss together with a
400 g (13 oz) can each of cannellini beans and butter
beans, rinsed and drained, 125 g (4 oz) halved baby
tomatoes, 4 sliced spring onions and 2 tablespoons
chopped parsley. Whisk together 3 tablespoons olive oil,
2 teaspoons truffle oil, 1 tablespoon balsamic vinegar
and 1 teaspoon clear honey, pour over the salad and
toss to serve. **Total cooking time 10 minutes.**

beetroot & goats' cheese salad

Serves **4**
Total cooking time **10 minutes**

2 tablespoons **olive oil**
3 **raw beetroot**, peeled and
   grated
4 tablespoons **balsamic
   vinegar**
2 tablespoons **sunflower
   seeds**
200 g (7 oz) **goats' cheese**
75 g (3 oz) **rocket leaves**
2 tablespoons **extra virgin
   olive oil**
pepper

Heat the olive oil in a frying pan, add the beetroot and cook for 3–4 minutes. Season well with pepper, then stir in the vinegar and cook over a high heat for 30 seconds.

Meanwhile, heat a nonstick frying pan over a medium-low heat and dry-fry the sunflower seeds for 2 minutes, stirring frequently, until golden and toasted. Set aside.

Divide the beetroot between 4 plates. Crumble over the cheese and top with the rocket.

Serve drizzled with the extra virgin olive oil and sprinkled with the toasted sunflower seeds.

For beetroot soup with goats' cheese, heat 1 tablespoon olive oil in a saucepan, add 1 chopped onion and cook for 2–3 minutes. Add 3 grated raw beetroot, 600 ml (1 pint) hot vegetable stock and a 400 g (13 oz) can chopped tomatoes and bring to the boil. Reduce the heat and simmer for 8–10 minutes until the beetroot is tender. Using a hand-held blender or food processor, blend the soup until smooth, then season to taste. Ladle into bowls and crumble over 100 g (3½ oz) goats' cheese to serve. **Total cooking time 20 minutes.**

cream of pumpkin & apple soup

Serves **4**
Total cooking time **30 minutes**

2 tablespoons **olive oil**
1 **onion**, chopped
600 g (1 lb 5 oz) **pumpkin flesh**, cut into chunks
1 **Bramley apple**, peeled, cored and chopped
2 **tomatoes**, skinned and chopped
900 ml (1½ pints) **vegetable stock**
100 ml (3½ fl oz) **double cream**
1 tablespoon finely chopped **flat leaf parsley**
salt and **pepper**

Heat the olive oil in a large saucepan and sauté the onion for 3–4 minutes.

Add the pumpkin and stir to coat with the onions. Stir in the apple and the chopped tomatoes.

Pour in the stock, bring to the boil and then simmer, covered, for 20 minutes, until the pumpkin is tender.

Leave the soup to cool a little before pouring in the cream. Using a hand blender, or in a food processor or blender, blend the soup until smooth.

Gently reheat if necessary, season and serve immediately, sprinkled with chopped parsley.

For pumpkin & chickpea salad, cut 1 kg (2 lb) pumpkin flesh into small dice. Toss with 1 crushed garlic clove, ½ teaspoon ground cumin and 2 tablespoons olive oil and roast in a preheated oven, 200°C (400°F), Gas Mark 6, for 15 minutes. Mix the roasted pumpkin with a 400 g (13 oz) can chickpeas, rinsed and drained, 1 small diced red onion, 150 g (5 oz) crumbled feta cheese, 50 g (2 oz) sun-dried tomatoes and 50 g (2 oz) rocket leaves. Serve dressed with shop-bought Italian salad dressing. **Total cooking time 20 minutes.**

watermelon & haloumi salad

Serves **4**
Total cooking time **10 minutes**

200 g (7 oz) **haloumi cheese**,
  cut into **8** slices
finely grated zest and juice of
  1 lime
2 **spring onions**, finely sliced
2 tablespoons chopped **flat
  leaf parsley**
2 tablespoons chopped **mint**
1 tablespoon **avocado oil**
150 g (5 oz) **wild rocket
  leaves**
½ **watermelon**, peeled,
  deseeded and diced
½ small **red onion**, finely
  sliced
100 g (3½ oz) **almond-
  stuffed green olives**
1 tablespoon **pomegranate
  molasses**
1–2 teaspoons **chilli paste**,
  to taste
100 g (3½ oz) **pomegranate
  seeds** (about 1 pomegranate)
pepper

Preheat the grill. Toss the haloumi with the lime zest, spring onions and 1 tablespoon each of the parsley and mint, then place on a foil-lined baking tray. Drizzle over a little of the avocado oil and place the tray under the grill for 3–4 minutes until hot and golden, turning once.

Meanwhile, arrange the rocket leaves on 4 large plates. Toss the watermelon, onion, olives and remaining parsley and mint in a large bowl. Spoon the dressed watermelon over the rocket.

In a small bowl, mix together the lime juice, pomegranate molasses, the remaining avocado oil and chilli paste, to taste, then season with black pepper.

Top each salad with 2 slices of the grilled haloumi, then scatter over the pomegranate seeds. Serve drizzled with the dressing.

For watermelon & feta salad, peel, deseed and dice ½ watermelon and arrange on serving plates. Crumble 200 g (7 oz) feta over the watermelon, then scatter 2 finely sliced spring onions, 2 tablespoons each of chopped mint and parsley and 100 g (3½ oz) black olives. Sprinkle over 100 g (3½ oz) pomegranate seeds and serve drizzled with 1 tablespoon pomegranate molasses. **Total cooking time 10 minutes.**

spicy soya bean & noodle salad

Serves **4**

Total cooking time **15 minutes**

250 g (8 oz) **dried soba noodles**

250 g (8 oz) **frozen podded soya beans**

6 **spring onions**, thinly sliced diagonally

2 tablespoons **sesame seeds**

3 cm (1 inch) piece of **fresh root ginger**

1 **red chilli**, finely chopped

1 tablespoon **toasted sesame oil**

3 tablespoons **mirin**

3 tablespoons **light soy sauce**

1 teaspoon **clear honey**

salt

chopped **fresh coriander leaves**, to garnish

Cook the noodles and soya beans in a large saucepan of lightly salted boiling water for 4–5 minutes, or according to the noodle packet instructions. Drain well, then return to the pan and add the spring onions. Cover and keep warm.

Heat a frying pan until hot, add the sesame seeds and dry-fry over a medium heat until lightly golden, then remove from the pan and set aside.

Peel and grate the root ginger into a bowl, then stir in the remaining ingredients and mix well. Pour the dressing over the noodle mixture and toss to mix well.

Ladle into warm bowls, scatter over the sesame seeds and chopped coriander and serve.

For soya bean, ginger, chilli & noodle broth, put 800 ml (1 pint 8 fl oz) hot vegetable stock, 1 teaspoon peeled and grated fresh root ginger, 1 chopped red chilli and 6 finely sliced spring onions in a saucepan and bring to the boil, then add 400 g (12 oz) shop-bought ready-cooked soba noodles and 200 g (7 oz) frozen podded soya beans. Bring back to the boil, then season and serve sprinkled with chopped fresh coriander leaves and a drizzle of sesame oil. **Total cooking time 10 minutes.**

bulgar & goats' cheese salad

Serves **4**
Total cooking time **20 minutes**

750 ml (1 ¼ pints) **hot
 vegetable stock**
275 g (9 oz) **bulgar wheat**
4 tablespoons **olive** or
 vegetable oil
1 large **red onion**, halved and
 thinly sliced
100 ml (3½ fl oz) **tomato juice**
2 tablespoons **lime juice**
175 g (6 oz) **firm goats'
 cheese**, crumbled
3 tablespoons roughly
 chopped **flat leaf parsley**
salt and **pepper**

Bring the vegetable stock to the boil in a large saucepan,
add the bulgar wheat and cook for 7 minutes. Remove
from the heat, cover with a tight-fitting lid and set aside
for 5–8 minutes, until the liquid has been absorbed and
the grains are tender.

Meanwhile, heat 2 tablespoons of oil in a frying pan
and cook the onion gently for 7–8 minutes, until soft
and golden.

Combine the remaining oil with the tomato juice and
lime juice, and season with salt and pepper. Fold the
dressing, onion, goats' cheese and parsley into the
bulgar wheat with a fork, and spoon into 4 shallow
bowls to serve.

For goats' cheese couscous, place 250 g (8 oz)
couscous in a bowl with 1 tablespoon of olive or
vegetable oil and a generous pinch of salt. Pour
over 300 ml (½ pint) boiling vegetable stock and set
aside for 5–8 minutes, until the grains are tender and
the liquid has been absorbed. Meanwhile, combine
3 tablespoons oil with 100 ml (3½ fl oz) tomato juice
and 2 tablespoons lime juice, and season with salt and
pepper. Fold the goats' cheese and parsley into the
couscous and spoon into serving bowls. Drizzle with
the dressing and scatter with 3 sliced spring onions
to serve. **Total cooking time 10 minutes.**

quinoa & tomato salad with feta

Serves **4**
Total cooking time **30 minutes**

150 g (5 oz) **quinoa**, rinsed
under running cold water
300 ml (½ pint) **boiling water**
4 **yellow** or **red tomatoes**,
deseeded and diced
1 large **green pepper**,
deseeded and finely
chopped
2 **spring onions**, finely sliced
100 g (3½ oz) **pitted**
Kalamata olives, roughly
chopped
½ **cucumber**, cut in half
lengthways, deseeded
and sliced
grated rind and juice of
1 **lemon**
3 tablespoons chopped **flat**
leaf parsley
3 tablespoons chopped **mint**
4 small **red** or **white chicory**,
sliced
100 g (3½ oz) **feta cheese**
2 tablespoons **toasted mixed**
seeds
small handful of **alfalfa**
sprouts
salt and **pepper**
lemon wedges, to serve

Tip the quinoa into a medium-sized saucepan and pour over the measured boiling water. Cover the pan and simmer gently for about 12–15 minutes. It is ready when the seed begins to come away from the germ. Drain the quinoa in a fine sieve and cool under running cold water. Drain well.

Meanwhile, mix together in a large bowl the tomatoes, pepper, spring onions, olives and cucumber, then stir in the lemon rind, parsley and mint.

Mix the cooled quinoa through the vegetables and season with salt, pepper and lemon juice, to taste. Set aside for 5–10 minutes to allow the flavours to develop.

Scatter the chicory onto 4 serving plates, spoon over the quinoa salad and crumble over the feta. Sprinkle with the toasted seeds and alfalfa sprouts and serve.

For minted pea quinoa, heat 250 g (8 oz) ready-to-eat red and white quinoa or ready-to-eat red mixed wholesome grains, according to the pack instructions. Tip the quinoa or grains into a bowl and toss with 3 tablespoons each of chopped flat leaf parsley and mint, 125 g (4 oz) thawed frozen peas and 2 finely sliced spring onions. Season with salt, pepper and lemon juice, to taste, and crumble over 100 g (3½ oz) Wensleydale cheese or a similar crumbly white cheese. Sprinkle over 2 tablespoons toasted mixed seeds and serve. **Total cooking time 10 minutes.**

panzanella

Serves **4**
Total cooking time **30 minutes**

300 g (10 oz) **ripe tomatoes**
125 g (4 oz) **ciabatta bread**
16 **black olives**, pitted
3 teaspoons **capers**
½ **red onion**, finely sliced
300 g (10 oz) **red** and **yellow
    cherry tomatoes**, halved
6–8 **basil leaves**
1 tablespoon **red wine
    vinegar**
2 tablespoons **olive oil**

Place the tomatoes in a sieve over a bowl. Using the back of a spoon, squash them well to release all the juice into the bowl.

Roughly break up the bread and add it to the tomato juice. Leave to stand for 15 minutes, then transfer to a serving dish.

Scatter the remaining ingredients over the soaked bread, drizzling over the red wine vinegar and olive oil before serving.

For tomato salad with ciabatta croûtons, cut
1 ciabatta loaf into cubes. Heat 2 tablespoons olive oil in a frying pan and fry the cubes of bread until they are golden. Drain on kitchen paper. Toss the fried bread together with 300 g (10 oz) roughly chopped ripe tomatoes, 16 pitted black olives, ½ sliced red onion, 300 g (10 oz) red and yellow cherry tomatoes, 6–8 basil leaves and 60 g (2¼ oz) baby spinach leaves. Drizzle with 2 tablespoons olive oil and 1 tablespoon red wine vinegar to serve.
Total cooking time 10 minutes.

chickpea, tomato & pepper salad

Serves **4**

Total cooking time **30 minutes**

3 large **red peppers**, cored, deseeded and cut into quarters

6 **plum tomatoes**, halved

4 tablespoons **olive oil**

1 teaspoon **cumin seeds**

1 tablespoon **lemon juice**

½ teaspoon **Dijon mustard**

½ teaspoon **clear honey**

400 g (13 oz) **can chickpeas**, drained

10–12 **basil leaves**, roughly torn

100 g (3½ oz) **baby spinach leaves**

salt and **pepper**

Place the peppers and tomatoes in a roasting tin and toss with 1 tablespoon of the oil and the cumin seeds. Season with salt and pepper and roast in a preheated oven, 220°C (425°F), Gas Mark 7, for 20 minutes.

Whisk the remaining oil with the lemon juice, mustard and honey to make a dressing.

Remove the peppers from the oven and spoon into a bowl. Stir in the chickpeas, basil and spinach, pour over the dressing and serve immediately.

For chickpea, tomato & pepper soup, heat 1 tablespoon olive oil in a large saucepan over a medium heat, add 1 deseeded and chopped red pepper and 1 diced red onion and cook for 1–2 minutes. Stir in a 400 g (13 oz) can of chickpeas, rinsed and drained, and 3 chopped plum tomatoes. Pour in 900 ml (1½ pints) vegetable stock and season well. Simmer for 4–5 minutes. Using a hand-held blender or food processor, blend until smooth and serve with a drizzle of olive oil. **Total cooking time 10 minutes.**

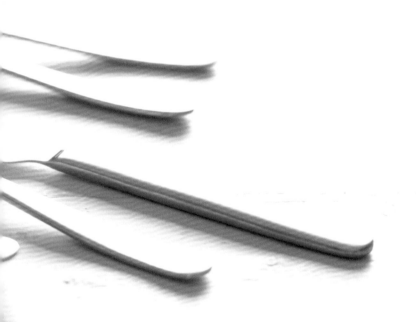

midweek
meals

asparagus & pea quinoa risotto

Serves **4**
Total cooking time **20 minutes**

275 g (9 oz) **quinoa**, rinsed
600 ml (1 pint) **hot vegetable stock**
200 g (7 oz) **asparagus**, chopped
200 g (7 oz) **frozen peas**
1 tablespoon chopped **mint**
3 tablespoons grated **Italian-style hard cheese**
pepper

Place the quinoa and stock in a saucepan and bring to the boil, then reduce the heat and simmer for 12–15 minutes until the quinoa is cooked, adding the asparagus and peas about 2 minutes before the end of the cooking time.

Drain the quinoa and vegetables, then return to the pan with the mint and 2 tablespoons of the cheese and season with pepper. Mix well.

Serve sprinkled with the remaining Italian-style hard cheese.

For asparagus & pea tart, unroll a 375 g (12 oz) pack ready-rolled puff pastry and place on a baking sheet. Mix together 200 g (7 oz) cream cheese and 1 tablespoon Dijon mustard in a bowl, then spread over the pastry, leaving a 1.5 cm (¾ inch) border around the edge. Top with 300 g (10 oz) trimmed asparagus and 100 g (3½ oz) defrosted peas. Drizzle with 2 tablespoons olive oil, then season with pepper and sprinkle with 50 g (2 oz) grated Italian-style hard cheese. Place in a preheated oven, 200°C (400°F), Gas Mark 6, for 20–22 minutes. Serve with a crisp green salad. **Total cooking time 30 minutes.**

crispy spinach & feta pie

Serves **4**
Total cooking time **30 minutes**

250 g (8 oz) **frozen leaf
  spinach**
2 **spring onions**, chopped
1 **garlic clove**, crushed
200 g (7 oz) **feta cheese**,
  crumbled
2 **eggs**, beaten
pinch of **grated nutmeg**
25 g (1 oz) **butter**, melted
3 tablespoons **olive oil**
5 large **filo pastry sheets**
salt and **pepper**

Place the spinach in a sieve, then pour over boiling water from the kettle to defrost. Squeeze to remove excess water, then mix with the spring onions, garlic, feta and eggs. Add the nutmeg and season to taste.

Stir together the butter and oil and brush over the sides and base of a 20 cm (8 inch) springform cake tin. Unwrap the filo pastry and cover with a piece of damp kitchen paper until ready to use it.

Working quickly, brush 1 sheet with the butter mixture and arrange in the tin, letting the excess pastry hang over the sides. Brush another sheet with the butter mixture, turn the tin a little and arrange it in the same way. Repeat until the bottom and sides of the tin are completely covered.

Spoon the filling into the tin, then fold the pastry edges over to cover the filling, scrunching them up a bit as you go. Brush the top of the pie with a little more butter mixture and cook in a preheated oven, 200°C (400°F), Gas Mark 6, for 20–25 minutes until golden and crisp.

For spinach, feta & chickpea salad, whisk together 1 tablespoon lemon juice, 3 tablespoons olive oil and a pinch of ground cumin. Toss with a 400 g (13 oz) can chickpeas, rinsed and drained, and ½ thinly sliced red onion and season well. Stir in 125 g (4 oz) baby spinach leaves and 1 chopped ready-roasted red pepper and arrange on a serving plate. Crumble over 75 g (3 oz) feta cheese and serve. **Total cooking time 10 minutes.**

quick spiced cauliflower pilau

Serves **4**
Total cooking time **10 minutes**

25 g (1 oz) **raisins**
400 g (13 oz) small
   cauliflower florets
2 tablespoons **vegetable oil**
2 **garlic cloves**, crushed
2 **spring onions**, thinly sliced
1 ½ tablespoons **medium-hot
   curry paste**
500 g (1 lb) **ready-cooked
   steamed pilau rice**
chopped **fresh coriander
   leaves**, to garnish
flatbreads, to serve (optional)

Put the raisins into a heatproof bowl, pour in 2 tablespoons boiling water and set aside to soak.

Cook the cauliflower florets in a large pan of boiling water for 4–5 minutes, until just tender.

Meanwhile, heat the oil in a large pan and fry the garlic and spring onions over a medium heat for 1 minute to soften. Add the curry paste and stir for 1 minute to cook the spices. Add the steamed rice, the raisins and their water, then cover and cook over a medium-low heat for 2–3 minutes.

Drain the cauliflower and fold it into the rice. Spoon into dishes, garnish with the coriander and serve accompanied by flatbreads, if desired.

For aromatic spiced cauliflower stew, heat 2 tablespoons vegetable oil in a pan and cook 1 chopped onion, 2 chopped garlic cloves and 1 teaspoon cumin seeds over a medium heat for 6–7 minutes, stirring occasionally, until softened. Add 2 tablespoons medium-hot curry paste and stir for 1 minute. Add 625 g (1 ¼ lb) cauliflower florets and a 400 g (13 oz) can rinsed and drained chickpeas and stir. Pour in a 400 g (13 oz) can cherry or plum tomatoes plus 200 ml (7 fl oz) water, then season, cover loosely and simmer for 15–18 minutes, until tender. Serve scattered with chopped fresh coriander leaves and a dollop of natural yogurt. **Total cooking time 30 minutes.**

ranch-style eggs

Serves **4**
Total cooking time **30 minutes**

2 tablespoons **olive oil**
1 **onion**, finely sliced
1 **red chilli**, deseeded and
  finely chopped
1 **garlic clove**, crushed
1 teaspoon **ground cumin**
1 teaspoon **dried oregano**
400 g (13 oz) **can cherry
  tomatoes**
200 g (7 oz) **roasted red and
  yellow peppers in oil** from
  a jar, drained and roughly
  chopped
4 **eggs**
salt and **pepper**
4 tablespoons finely chopped
  fresh coriander, to garnish

Heat the oil in a large frying pan and add the onion, chilli, garlic, cumin and oregano.

Fry gently for about 5 minutes or until soft, then add the tomatoes and peppers and cook for a further 5 minutes. If the sauce looks dry, add a splash of water. Season well.

Make 4 hollows in the mixture, break an egg into each and cover the pan. Cook for 5 minutes or until the eggs are just set.

Serve immediately, garnished with chopped coriander.

For spicy Mexican-style scrambled eggs, heat 1 tablespoon each olive oil and butter in a large frying pan. Whisk together 8 eggs with 1 crushed garlic clove, 1 finely chopped red chilli, 1 teaspoon dried oregano and 1 teaspoon ground cumin. Season, pour into the frying pan and cook over a medium-low heat, stirring often or until the eggs are scrambled and cooked to your liking. Serve with warm tortillas and garnish with chopped fresh coriander. **Total cooking time 10 minutes.**

potato gnocchi

Serves **4**

Total cooking time **30 minutes**

800 g (1¾ lb) **floury
    potatoes**, peeled and diced
1 **egg yolk**, beaten
150 g (5 oz) **plain flour**
15 g (½ oz) **basil leaves**,
    finely shredded
50 g (2 oz) **Italian-style hard
    cheese**, grated
4 tablespoons **extra-virgin
    olive oil**
salt and **pepper**

Cook the potatoes in a saucepan of boiling water for 12–15 minutes, until soft. Drain and mash, or use a potato ricer to get a really smooth texture. Place another saucepan of water on the heat to boil.

Transfer the mashed potato to a bowl and mix in the egg yolk, flour and basil. Mix well to combine.

Take a teaspoon of the mixture into your hand and roll into a walnut-sized ball. Press with the prongs of a fork to make a gnocchi shape. Repeat with the remaining mixture.

Drop the gnocchi into the saucepan of boiling water to cook – this should take only 1–2 minutes and the gnocchi will float when cooked.

Toss the hot gnocchi in the grated cheese and olive oil and serve immediately.

For potato gnocchi in a quick tomato sauce, heat 1 tablespoon olive oil in a frying pan and sauté 2 diced shallots and 2 crushed garlic cloves for 1–2 minutes. Add a 400 g (13 oz) can chopped tomatoes, a pinch of dried chilli flakes, 2 teaspoons thyme leaves and 2 tablespoons white wine. Simmer for 5–6 minutes. Meanwhile, cook 800 g (1¾ lb) ready-made gnocchi for 2 minutes in a saucepan of boiling water. Drain and toss the cooked gnocchi in the tomato sauce and serve sprinkled with Italian-style hard cheese shavings. **Total cooking time 10 minutes.**

coconut dahl with toasted naan

Serves **4**
Total cooking time **10 minutes**

1 tablespoon **vegetable oil**
1 **onion**, roughly chopped
2 tablespoons **korma curry paste**
125 g (4 oz) **split red lentils**, rinsed
400 g (13 oz) **can coconut milk**
black pepper
chopped **fresh coriander**
naan breads

Heat the oil in a heavy-based saucepan and cook the onion over a high heat, stirring, for 1 minute, then stir in the curry paste and lentils.

Pour in the coconut milk, then fill the can with water and add to the lentils. Simmer briskly, uncovered, for 8–9 minutes until the lentils are tender and the mixture is thick and pulpy. Season with black pepper and sprinkle over the chopped coriander.

Meanwhile, lightly toast the naan breads under a preheated high grill until warm and golden. Cut into fingers and serve alongside the dahl for dipping.

For chunky vegetable dahl with toasted naan fingers, heat 4 tablespoons vegetable oil in a large saucepan and cook 1 roughly chopped onion, 1 trimmed and roughly chopped large courgette and 1 trimmed and roughly chopped aubergine over a medium-high heat, stirring occasionally, for 10 minutes until tender. Stir in 4 tablespoons korma curry paste and 125 g (4 oz) rinsed split red lentils, then pour in 600 ml (1 pint) vegetable stock and simmer for 10–15 minutes until thick and pulpy. Meanwhile, prepare the toasted naan fingers as above and serve with the dahl. **Total cooking time 30 minutes.**

courgette & feta fritters

Serves **4**
Total cooking time **20 minutes**

1 **egg**, lightly beaten
25 g (1 oz) **self-raising flour**
2 tablespoons **buttermilk**
2 **large courgettes**, grated
handful of **dill**, chopped
3 **spring onions**, chopped
150 g (5 oz) **feta cheese**
75 ml (3 fl oz) **olive oil**
toasted **pitta breads**, to serve

Pepper salad
2 **ready-roasted peppers**
  from a jar, chopped
1 tablespoon **lemon juice**
2 tablespoons **olive oil**
handful of **mint leaves**,
  chopped

Mix together the egg, flour and buttermilk until smooth. Place the courgettes in a clean tea towel and squeeze to remove excess water, then mix into the batter along with the dill and spring onions. Crumble in the feta.

Heat half the oil in a large nonstick frying pan. Add heaped tablespoons of the mixture to the pan and press down a little on each fritter with the back of the spoon to flatten slightly. Cook for 3 minutes until golden brown, then turn and cook for 2 minutes more until golden and cooked through. Drain on kitchen paper and keep warm. Repeat with the remaining mixture and oil.

Stir together the roasted peppers, lemon juice, oil and mint. Serve alongside the fritters with some toasted pitta breads.

For tangy couscous, courgette & feta salad, slice 2 courgettes into long, thin strips. Rub with 2 tablespoons olive oil and cook on a hot griddle pan for 1 minute on each side until lightly charred. Place 300 g (10 oz) couscous in a bowl and pour over 400 ml (14 fl oz) hot vegetable stock. Cover and leave for 5 minutes, then stir in 4 tablespoons lemon juice, 5 tablespoons olive oil and a handful each of chopped parsley and mint. Season and add 75 g (3 oz) sun-blush tomatoes and the courgettes. Scatter over 50 g (2 oz) toasted pine nuts and 100 g (3½ oz) crumbled feta cheese. **Total cooking time 10 minutes.**

tomato risotto

Serves **4**
Total cooking time **30 minutes**

1 tablespoon **olive oil**
1 **onion**, diced
2 **garlic cloves**, crushed
100 g (3½ oz) **plum tomatoes**
200 ml (7 fl oz) **ready-made tomato sauce**
300 ml (½ pint) **hot vegetable stock**
200 g (7 oz) **Arborio rice**
50 g (2 oz) **sun-dried tomatoes**, cut into strips
2 tablespoons shredded **basil leaves**
salt and **pepper**
40 g (1¾ oz) grated **Italian-style hard cheese**, to serve

Heat the olive oil in a saucepan and sauté the onion and garlic for 5–6 minutes.

Meanwhile, place the tomatoes in a large bowl and pour over boiling water. Leave to stand for 30 seconds, then drain and refresh under cold water. Peel off the skins, then deseed and chop the tomatoes.

Place the tomato sauce and stock in a small saucepan and bring to a simmer.

Stir the rice into the onions and continue to stir, for 1–2 minutes until the edges of the grains look translucent.

Add a ladle of the tomato sauce and stock and stir continuously, until it has all been absorbed. Repeat with the remaining hot stock, adding a ladle at a time, until the rice is 'al dente'.

Stir in the chopped tomatoes, sliced sun-dried tomatoes and basil and season to taste.

Serve sprinkled with grated Italian-style hard cheese.

For quick tomato & rice salad, skin and chop 4 plum tomatoes, as above, and mix with 4 sliced spring onions, 400 g (13 oz) shop-bought ready-cooked rice, 200 g (7 oz) diced mozzarella cheese and 2 tablespoons chopped basil leaves. Season and sprinkle with 2 tablespoons olive oil to serve. **Total cooking time 10 minutes**.

cheese & spinach calzones

Serves **4**
Total cooking time **30 minutes**

500 g (1 lb) **strong bread
    flour**, plus extra for dusting
1 x 7-g (¼-oz) **sachet dried
    yeast**
a pinch of **salt**
3 tablespoons **olive oil**
300 ml (½ pint) **warm water**
300 g (10 oz) **spinach**
400 g (13 oz) **ricotta cheese**
4 tablespoons grated **Italian-
    style hard cheese**
4 tablespoons grated
    **vegetarian Pecorino-style
    cheese**
4 **spring onions**, sliced
1 teaspoon **freshly ground
    black pepper**

To make the dough, place the flour, yeast and salt in a large bowl and mix together. Make a well in the centre. Stir in 1 tablespoon of the olive oil and most of the measured water. Mix together with your hand, gradually adding more water if necessary, until you have a soft, but not sticky dough.

Turn the dough out on to a floured work surface and knead for 5–10 minutes until the dough is smooth and elastic. Divide into 4 pieces and roll each out to 20 cm (8 inch) circles.

Heat the remaining olive oil in a frying pan, add the spinach and cook for 2–3 minutes, until it has completely wilted. Place in a bowl and stir in the remaining ingredients.

Divide the mixture between the 4 circles of dough, placing the mixture on one half of each circle, leaving a 2.5 cm (1 inch) clean edge. Brush the clean edges with water, then fold the other half over the filling and pinch the edges together to seal. Place the calzones on a baking sheet and bake in a preheated oven, 220°C (425°F), Gas Mark 7, for 6–8 minutes, until the dough is cooked and the filling is hot.

For cheese & spinach stuffed pitta breads, heat 1 tablespoon olive oil in a frying pan and sauté 1 sliced red onion for a few minutes, then add 250 g (8 oz) spinach leaves and stir to wilt. Take off the heat and mix with 4 tablespoons grated Italian-style hard cheese and 200 g (7 oz) torn mozzarella. Heat 4 pitta breads, slice along one side and open up. Fill each pitta with the spinach filling. **Total cooking time 10 minutes.**

feta, spring onion & walnut tartlets

Serves **4**

Total cooking time **10 minutes**

4 slices of **brown bread**,
   crusts removed
150 g (5 oz) **feta cheese**,
   crumbled
2 **spring onions**, thinly sliced
25 g (1 oz) **walnut pieces**,
   lightly crushed
8 **cherry tomatoes**, cut into
   quarters
1 tablespoon **olive oil**
salt and **pepper**

To serve

200 g (7 oz) **mixed salad
   leaves**
½ **cucumber**, sliced

Roll the bread out thinly using a rolling pin. Cut each slice into a circle, approximately 12 cm (5 inches) in diameter and press the circles into 4 large nonstick muffin or Yorkshire pudding tins. Cook in a preheated oven to 200°C (400°F), Gas Mark 6, for 7–8 minutes, until crisp and golden.

Meanwhile, mix the crumbled feta with the spring onions, walnut pieces and tomatoes. Season to taste, then spoon the mixture into the toasted tart cases. Drizzle with the olive oil and serve with a mixed leaf and cucumber salad.

For feta, spring onion & walnut tart, Roll 500 g (1 lb) ready-made puff pastry into a rectangle measuring approximately 30 x 20 cm (12 x 8 inches). Place on a lightly greased baking sheet and score a border about 1.5 cm (¾ inch) in from the edges all the way around the pastry, not quite cutting through. Scatter 200 g (7 oz) crumbled feta, 4 thinly sliced spring onions, 50 g (2 oz) walnut pieces and 12 quartered cherry tomatoes over the pastry, keeping within the border. Drizzle with 1 tablespoon olive oil and cook in a preheated oven, 200°C (400°F), Gas Mark 6, for about 20 minutes until crisp and golden. Serve with salad. **Total cooking time 30 minutes.**

delicatessen pasta

Serves **4**
Total cooking time **20 minutes**

375 g (12 oz) **fusilli**
2 tablespoons **extra virgin olive oil**
1 tablespoon **balsamic vinegar**
½ teaspoon **Dijon mustard**
½ teaspoon **clear honey**
1 **garlic clove**, crushed
10 **sun-dried tomatoes**, sliced
400 g (13 oz) **can artichoke hearts**, drained and halved
100 g (3½ oz) **Italian-style hard cheese** shavings

Cook the fusilli in a pan of boiling water for 9–12 minutes, or according to the pack instructions.

Whisk together the oil, vinegar, mustard, honey and garlic to make the dressing.

Drain the pasta and return to the pan with the dressing. Stir in the sun-dried tomatoes and artichoke hearts and stir to warm through.

Serve in shallow pasta bowls, sprinkled with the Italian-style hard cheese shavings.

For artichoke & sun-dried tomato bruschetta, slice 2 baguettes into 16 slices and place on a baking sheet. Drizzle with 2 tablespoons olive oil and toast for 2–3 minutes on each side. Rub one side of each slice with a peeled garlic clove. Top the bruschetta with a 400 g (13 oz) can artichoke hearts, drained and sliced and 12 chopped sun-dried tomatoes. Serve sprinkled with 2 tablespoons toasted pine nuts and small basil leaves. **Total cooking time 10 minutes.**

moroccan vegetable tagine

Serves **4**
Total cooking time **30 minutes**

200 g (7 oz) **couscous**
550 ml (18 fl oz) **boiling water**
2 tablespoons **sunflower oil**
1 large **onion**, finely chopped
2 **garlic cloves**, minced
1 teaspoon grated **fresh root ginger**
2 teaspoons **ground cumin**
1 teaspoon **ground coriander**
2 teaspoons **ground cinnamon**
1 teaspoon **ground turmeric**
2 teaspoons **dried red chilli flakes**
1 tablespoon **harissa paste**
400 g (13 oz) **can chopped tomatoes**
250 ml (8 fl oz) **hot vegetable stock**
2 **red peppers**, cored, deseeded and cut into bite-sized pieces
700 g (1½ lb) **butternut squash**, peeled, deseeded and cubed
100 g (3½ oz) **golden sultanas**
salt and **pepper**
chopped **fresh coriander**, to garnish

Put the couscous in a large heatproof bowl and season with salt. Pour over the measured water, cover with cling film and leave to stand for 10 minutes, or according to the pack instructions, until the water is absorbed. Gently fork to separate the grains, then set aside and keep warm.

Meanwhile, heat the oil in a large frying pan, add the onion and cook over a medium heat, stirring occasionally, for 2–3 minutes until softened. Add the garlic, ginger, ground spices, chilli flakes, harissa, tomatoes and stock and bring to the boil, then reduce the heat to low, cover and simmer gently for 10–12 minutes.

Stir in the red peppers, squash and sultanas, re-cover and increase the heat to medium. Simmer for 10–15 minutes or until the vegetables are tender, then season to taste.

Spoon the couscous into warm bowls, then ladle over the tagine and serve scattered with chopped coriander.

For Moroccan kebabs, cut 2 large courgettes, 2 cored and deseeded red peppers and 1 aubergine into chunks and place in a large bowl. Mix together 8 tablespoons olive oil, 1 tablespoon harissa paste, the juice of 2 lemons and a small handful of chopped coriander, pour over the vegetables and toss. Thread the veg onto 12 metal skewers, season and cook under a preheated medium grill for 10–12 minutes, turning once. Serve with couscous. **Total cooking time 20 minutes.**

cheat's pepper pizza

Serves **4**

Total cooking time **10 minutes**

4 **pitta breads**

4 tablespoons **tomato ketchup**

4 **ready-roasted red and yellow peppers** from a jar, drained and sliced

4 **spring onions**, sliced

150 g (5 oz) **mozzarella cheese**, sliced

small handful of **rocket leaves**

Toast the pitta breads for 2 minutes on each side. Top each one with 1 tablespoon tomato ketchup and the roasted peppers, spring onions and mozzarella.

Place under a preheated hot grill and cook for 4–6 minutes, until bubbling and golden. Serve topped with the rocket.

For polenta pepper pizza, bring 1 litre (1¾ pints) water to the boil in a large saucepan. Slowly pour in 250 g (8 oz) polenta, stirring constantly. Add 1 teaspoon dried oregano, season and continue to cook, stirring, for 8–10 minutes, until the polenta is thick. Divide in half, pour out onto 2 lightly oiled baking sheets, and spread into a circle about 1 cm (½ inch) thick. Bake in a preheated oven, 200°C (400°F), Gas Mark 6, for 12 minutes. Spread 400 g (13 oz) can chopped tomatoes over the polenta, then top with 350 g (11½ oz) ready-roasted peppers, cut into strips, and 10–12 roughly torn basil leaves, then sprinkle with 250 g (8 oz) sliced mozzarella cheese. Bake for a further 12–15 minutes, until the cheese is golden and bubbling. Serve hot, cut into wedges. **Total cooking time 40 minutes.**

basil & rocket pesto spaghetti

Serves **4**
Total cooking time **20 minutes**

50 g (2 oz) **sunflower** or
   pumpkin seeds
500 g (1 lb) **wholewheat
   spaghetti**
1 **garlic clove**, roughly
   chopped
1 small bunch of **basil**
75 g (3 oz) **rocket leaves**
25 g (1 oz) **Italian-style hard
   cheese**, finely grated, plus
   extra to serve (optional)
6 tablespoons **olive oil**
1 tablespoon **lemon juice**
sea salt and **pepper**

Place the seeds in a small, dry frying pan and toast gently for 3–4 minutes, shaking the pan frequently, until lightly toasted and golden. Tip onto a plate to cool.

Cook the spaghetti in a large saucepan of lightly salted boiling water for 11–12 minutes, or according to the pack instructions, until 'al dente'.

Meanwhile, crush the garlic together with a generous pinch of sea salt using a pestle and mortar. Add the basil and rocket leaves, and pound until crushed to a coarse paste.

Add the toasted seeds and pound to a paste, then transfer to a bowl and stir in the cheese, olive oil and lemon juice. Season to taste with plenty of black pepper and more salt, if necessary.

Drain the pasta and toss immediately with the pesto. Divide between 4 shallow bowls and serve with extra cheese, if desired.

For creamy gnocchi pesto bake, cook 500 g (1 lb) ready-made gnocchi in a large saucepan of lightly salted boiling water for about 2 minutes, or according to pack instructions, until just tender. Meanwhile, mix together 4 tablespoons ready-made green pesto and 300 ml (½ pint) crème fraîche. Stir in the cooked gnocchi, then transfer to a large ovenproof dish and sprinkle with 2 tablespoons grated Italian-style hard cheese. Cook in a preheated oven, 190°C (375°F), Gas Mark 5, for about 20 minutes until bubbling and golden. Serve with extra rocket leaves, if desired. **Total cooking time 30 minutes.**

polenta chips with arrabbiata dip

Serves **2**
Total cooking time **10 minutes**

500 g (1 lb) **ready-made polenta**
3 tablespoons **plain flour**, for dusting
4 tablespoons **olive oil**
375 g (12 oz) carton **shop-bought arrabbiata pasta sauce**

To serve
rocket leaves
Italian-style hard cheese shavings

Cut the block of polenta into chip-shaped fingers and dust in the flour, shaking off the excess.

Heat the oil in a frying pan and cook the polenta chips over a medium-high heat for 2–3 minutes on each side, until crisp and golden. Drain on kitchen paper and keep warm.

Meanwhile, heat the arrabbiata sauce in a pan. Spoon into small bowls and serve with the polenta chips, rocket leaves and Italian-style hard cheese shavings.

For arrabbiata polenta bake, pour half a 375 g (12 oz) carton arrabbiata sauce into the bottom of a medium ovenproof dish. Lay 300 g (10 oz) sliced polenta over the sauce and top with 50 g (2 oz) diced mozzarella and 2 tablespoons grated Italian-style hard cheese. Pour over the remaining sauce and top with 75 g (3 oz) diced mozzarella and 2 tablespoons grated Italian-style hard cheese. Bake in a preheated oven, 220°C (425°F), Gas Mark 7, for 20–25 minutes, until golden and bubbling. Serve with a salad, as above. **Total cooking time 30 minutes.**

mediterranean beans

Serves **4**
Total cooking time **10 minutes**

2 tablespoons **extra virgin
olive oil**
1 **red onion**, diced
1 **garlic clove**, crushed
½ teaspoon **cumin seeds**
400 g (13 oz) **can cannellini
beans**, rinsed and drained
75 g (3 oz) **cherry tomatoes**,
quartered
2 teaspoons chopped **sage**
4 slices of **crusty bread**
salt and **pepper**
25 g (1 oz) **Manchego
cheese**, grated, to serve

Heat the oil in a large frying pan, add the onion and
cook for 1–2 minutes. Add the garlic and cumin seeds
and cook for a further 2–3 minutes.

Add the beans and mix well to allow them to soak up
the flavours, then add the tomatoes. Stir in the sage,
season with salt and pepper and heat through.

Meanwhile, toast the bread under a preheated hot grill
for 2–3 minutes on each side. Serve topped with the
beans and a sprinkling of cheese.

For mixed bean goulash, heat 1 tablespoon olive oil
in a large frying pan, add 1 large chopped onion and
2 crushed garlic cloves and gently fry for 5 minutes
until softened. Stir in 100 g (3½ oz) chopped chestnut
mushrooms and cook for a further 3–4 minutes. Add
1 tablespoon smoked paprika and continue to cook
for 1–2 minutes. Stir in a 400 g (13 oz) can chopped
tomatoes, 200 ml (7 fl oz) hot vegetable stock and
a 400 g (13 oz) can mixed beans, rinsed and drained.
Bring to the boil, then reduce the heat and simmer
for 12–14 minutes until thick and glossy. Serve with
cooked rice, topped with dollops of soured cream, if
liked. **Total cooking time 30 minutes.**

butternut & broccoli au gratin

Serves **4**
Total cooking time **20 minutes**

200 g (7 oz) **purple sprouting broccoli**, trimmed

300 g (10 oz) **butternut squash**, peeled, deseeded and chopped

200 g (7 oz) **mushrooms**, halved

60 g (2¼ oz) **butter**

2 tablespoons **plain flour**

400 ml (14 fl oz) **milk**

2 teaspoons **wholegrain mustard**

100 g (3½ oz) **Cheddar cheese**, grated

Steam the vegetables in a steamer for 8–10 minutes until tender.

Meanwhile, melt the butter in a small saucepan, then stir in the flour to make a roux. Cook for 1–2 minutes, then gradually whisk in the milk and cook, stirring continuously, until the sauce is thick and smooth. Stir in the mustard and half the grated cheese.

Transfer the vegetables to an ovenproof dish, pour over the sauce and sprinkle with the remaining cheese. Cook under a preheated hot grill for 5–6 minutes until bubbling and golden.

For cheesy butternut mash with broccoli & poached eggs, cook 400 g (13 oz) peeled, deseeded and diced butternut squash and 150 g (5 oz) peeled and diced potatoes in a saucepan of boiling water for 8 minutes until tender. Meanwhile, bring a saucepan of water to a gentle simmer and stir with a large spoon to create a swirl. Break 2 eggs into the water and cook for 3 minutes. Remove with a slotted spoon and keep warm. Repeat with another 2 eggs. In a separate pan, steam 400 g (13 oz) broccoli florets until tender. Drain the squash and potatoes, then mash in the pan with 75 g (3 oz) grated Cheddar cheese. Serve topped with the broccoli and poached eggs, sprinkled with 2 tablespoons grated Italian-style hard cheese. **Total cooking time 10 minutes.**

tomato & aubergine pappardelle

Serves **4**
Total cooking time **30 minutes**

4 tablespoons **extra virgin olive oil**
1 large **aubergine**, cut into 1.5 cm (¾ in) dice
1 small **onion**, finely diced
2 **garlic cloves**, crushed
1 x 350 g (11½ oz) **jar tomato and basil pasta sauce**
375 g (12 oz) **dried pappardelle** or **tagliatelle**
250 g (8 oz) **buffalo mozzarella cheese**, drained and diced
black pepper

To garnish (optional)
4 tablespoons grated **Italian-style hard cheese**
basil leaves, roughly torn

Heat the oil in a large frying pan over a medium-high heat. Add the aubergine and onion and cook, stirring, for 5 minutes.

Add the garlic and cook for 1 minute. Add the tomato sauce and 200 ml (7 fl oz) water to the pan, bring to a simmer and cook for 8–10 minutes, or until the aubergines are just tender. Season to taste.

Meanwhile, cook the pasta in boiling water according to the pack instructions. Remove from the heat, drain, and return to the pan.

Stir the mozzarella into the sauce until it begins to melt slightly, then add to the pasta. Toss to mix well and season with black pepper. Sprinkle over the grated Italian-style hard cheese and garnish with basil leaves, if liked.

For tomato, aubergine & mozzarella pizzas, place 2 ready-made pizza bases on 2 baking sheets and spread over the tomato and aubergine sauce from the above recipe. Scatter over 250 g (8 oz) diced mozzarella cheese and cook in a preheated oven 220°C (425°F), Gas Mark 7, for 8–10 minutes. Serve immediately. **Total cooking time 10 minutes.**

broad bean & feta tagliatelle

Serves **4**
Total cooking time **10 minutes**

325 g (11 oz) **tagliatelle**
300 g (10 oz) **fresh** or **frozen broad beans**
2 tablespoons **olive oil**
6 **spring onions**, sliced
½ teaspoon **dried chilli flakes**
75 g (3 oz) **watercress**, roughly chopped
grated rind of 1 **lemon**
200 g (7 oz) **feta cheese**, crumbled
2 tablespoons **toasted pine nuts**

Cook the pasta in a large saucepan of boiling water for 8–9 minutes, or according to the pack instructions, until 'al dente'. Add the broad beans 3 minutes before the end of the cooking time.

Meanwhile, heat the oil in a large frying pan, add the spring onions and chilli flakes and cook for 2–3 minutes. Stir in the watercress and lemon rind.

Drain the pasta and beans and add to the watercress mixture with the feta. Mix well.

Serve sprinkled with the toasted pine nuts.

For broad bean & feta salad, place 250 g (8 oz) couscous in a large heatproof bowl and just cover with boiling water. Leave to stand for 10–12 minutes. Meanwhile, cook 300 g (10 oz) frozen broad beans in a saucepan of boiling water for 4–5 minutes until tender, then drain. Heat 1 tablespoon olive oil in a frying pan, add 125 g (4 oz) baby spinach leaves and cook briefly until wilted. Fluff up the couscous with a fork, then stir in the broad beans, spinach, 2 tablespoons chopped mint, 75 g (3 oz) sliced pitted black olives and 200 g (7 oz) crumbled feta cheese. Whisk together the juice of ½ lemon and 2 tablespoons olive oil in a small bowl, then drizzle over the salad and serve. **Total cooking time 20 minutes.**

mixed mushroom stroganoff

Serves **4**
Total cooking time **20 minutes**

4 tablespoons **olive oil**
1 **onion**, finely chopped
375 g (12 oz) **chestnut
mushrooms**, trimmed
and quartered
175 g (6 oz) **shiitake
mushrooms**, trimmed
and halved
100 g (3½ oz) **oyster
mushrooms**, trimmed
and halved
1 tablespoon **brandy**
1 teaspoon **Dijon mustard**
200 ml (7 fl oz) **crème fraîche**
pepper

To serve
cooked brown or **white long-
grain rice**
4 tablespoons chopped
flat leaf parsley

Heat the oil in a large, heavy-based frying pan and
cook the onion over a medium heat, stirring frequently,
for 2–3 minutes until softened. Add the chestnut
mushrooms and cook, stirring frequently, for 5 minutes
until lightly browned. Add the shiitake and oyster
mushrooms and cook, stirring frequently, for 5 minutes
until softened.

Pour the brandy into the mushroom mixture and stir
over a high heat until evaporated. Mix the mustard into
the crème fraîche, then spoon into the pan and heat for
2 minutes until piping hot. Season well with pepper.

Serve the stroganoff over cooked brown or white long-
grain rice, with the parsley scattered over.

For mushroom stroganoff on wholegrain toast,
thickly slice 250 g (8 oz) trimmed chestnut mushrooms
and 250 g (8 oz) trimmed portobello mushrooms. Melt
25 g (1 oz) garlic butter in a large frying pan, add
the mushrooms and cook over a high heat, stirring
frequently, for 4–5 minutes. Meanwhile, toast and butter
4 thick slices of wholegrain bread. Stir 1 tablespoon
wholegrain mustard and 300 ml (½ pint) soured cream
into the mushrooms. Season to taste and serve on the
toast with 1 tablespoon chopped chives scattered over.
Total cooking time 10 minutes.

pasta with dolcelatte & spinach

Serves **4**
Total cooking time **20 minutes**

400 g (13 oz) **fettucine**
1 tablespoon **olive oil**
1 **onion**, chopped
2 **garlic cloves**, crushed
300 ml (½ pint) **single cream**
125 g (4 oz) **dolcelatte
cheese**
150 g (5 oz) **baby spinach
leaves**
salt and **pepper**

Cook the fettucine in a saucepan of boiling water according to the pack instructions, until 'al dente'.

Meanwhile, heat the olive oil in a frying pan and sauté the onion and garlic for 4–5 minutes. Add the cream and simmer for 5–6 minutes, until the cream thickens a little.

Stir in the dolcelatte and spinach and stir for 1 minute. Drain the pasta and add to the spinach. Season with salt and pepper, then gently mix together and serve in warmed bowls.

For dolcelatte & spinach soup, heat 1 tablespoon olive oil in a saucepan and sauté 1 chopped onion and 2 chopped garlic cloves for 3–4 minutes. Stir in 1 chopped potato and cook for a further 1–2 minutes. Pour in 450 ml (¾ pint) vegetable stock and bring to the boil. Simmer for 10 minutes, then stir in 600 ml (1 pint) milk and bring to a simmer again. Add 225 g (7½ oz) baby spinach leaves and the grated rind of 1 lemon and cook for 5–6 minutes, then stir in another 225 g (7½ oz) baby spinach leaves and 50 g (2 oz) dolcelatte. Using a hand blender, or in a food processor or blender, blend the soup until smooth. Season and serve the soup with toasted pumpkin seeds and a few more crumbs of dolcelatte. **Total cooking time 30 minutes.**

patatas bravas

Serves **4**
Total cooking time **30 minutes**

800 g (1¾ lb) **potatoes,**
   peeled and cut into small
   cubes
2 tablespoons **olive oil**
400 g (13 oz) **can chopped**
   tomatoes
1 small **red onion,** finely
   chopped
2 **garlic cloves,** finely chopped
1 teaspoon **dried red chilli**
   flakes
1 teaspoon **cayenne pepper**
3 teaspoons **sweet smoked**
   paprika
1 **bay leaf**
1 teaspoon **golden caster**
   sugar
salt and **pepper**
finely chopped **flat leaf**
   parsley, to garnish
crusty bread, to serve

Cook the potatoes in a large saucepan of salted boiling water for 10–12 minutes or until tender, then drain well.

Line a baking sheet with nonstick baking paper. Place the potatoes in a single layer on the sheet, drizzle over the oil and season. Place in a preheated oven, 220°C (425°F), Gas Mark 7, for 10–12 minutes or until lightly browned.

Meanwhile, put the tomatoes, red onion, garlic, chilli flakes and cayenne pepper in a saucepan and cook over a medium heat for 10 minutes, stirring occasionally, then stir in the paprika, bay leaf and sugar and cook for a further 4–5 minutes until thickened. Remove and discard the bay leaf.

Transfer the potatoes to a warm serving dish, then pour over the spicy tomato sauce and toss to mix well. Scatter with chopped parsley and serve with crusty bread.

For spicy potato & tomato stir-fry, heat 2 tablespoons sunflower oil in a large wok or frying pan until hot, add a drained 540 g (1 lb 3 oz) can new potatoes, cubed, 1 roughly chopped onion, 1 teaspoon dried red chilli flakes, 1 tablespoon sweet smoked paprika and 2 diced plum tomatoes and stir-fry over a high heat for 5–6 minutes or until piping hot, then season. Serve with a green salad and warm bread. **Total cooking time 10 minutes.**

lentil bolognese

Serves **4**

Total cooking time **30 minutes**

1 **onion**, roughly chopped
1 **carrot**, peeled and chopped
1 **celery stick**, roughly
  chopped
1 **garlic clove**, peeled
3 tablespoons **olive oil**
125 ml (4 fl oz) **red wine**
100 ml (3½ fl oz) **water**
75 g (3 oz) **tomato purée**
400 g (13 oz) **can chopped
  tomatoes**
1 teaspoon **dried mixed
  herbs**
2 x 400 g (13 oz) **cans green
  lentils**, drained and rinsed
salt and **pepper**

To serve
50 g (2 oz) grated **Italian-
  style hard cheese**
crusty bread

Place the onion, carrot, celery and garlic in a food processor and pulse briefly until finely chopped. Heat the olive oil in a large, heavy-based casserole or saucepan. Add the vegetable mixture and cook for 5–6 minutes, stirring frequently, until softened and lightly golden.

Pour in the red wine, measured water, tomato purée, chopped tomatoes and herbs, and season to taste with salt and pepper. Simmer gently for about 15 minutes, then add the lentils and simmer for a further 5–7 minutes, until thickened and tender. Spoon into deep bowls, sprinkle with cheese and serve with plenty of fresh, crusty bread.

For cheat's lentil Bolognese, place 1 roughly chopped onion, 1 peeled and roughly chopped carrot, 1 roughly chopped celery stick and 1 garlic clove in a food processor and pulse until finely chopped. Heat 3 tablespoons olive oil in a large, heavy-based casserole or saucepan and cook the vegetable mixture for 5–6 minutes, stirring frequently, until softened and lightly golden. Stir in a 500 g (1 lb) jar tomato pasta sauce and 2 x 400 g (13 oz) cans green lentils, drained and rinsed. Simmer gently for 2–3 minutes, then serve as above, with grated Italian-style hard cheese and crusty bread. **Total cooking time 10 minutes.**

hot & spicy

aubergine, tomato & chilli curry

Serves **4**

Total cooking time **30 minutes**

2 large **aubergines**
100 ml (3½ fl oz) **vegetable oil**
2 **onions**, very thinly sliced
6 **garlic cloves**, finely chopped
3 teaspoons peeled and grated finely chopped **fresh root ginger**
2 **red chillies**, deseeded and thinly sliced
200 g (7 oz) **canned chopped tomatoes**
6 **kaffir lime leaves**
1 tablespoon **ketjap manis (thick soy sauce)**
2 tablespoons **dark soy sauce**
1 teaspoon **soft light brown sugar**
juice of **1 lime**
small handful of chopped **fresh coriander leaves**
2 tablespoons chopped **roasted peanuts**
steamed noodles or **rice**, to serve

Cut the aubergines into finger-thick batons. Reserve 1 tablespoon of the oil, then heat the remaining oil in a large frying pan, add the aubergines and fry over a medium heat, stirring occasionally, for 5–6 minutes or until lightly browned. Remove with a slotted spoon and drain on kitchen paper.

Heat the reserved oil in the pan, add the onions and garlic and cook over a medium heat, stirring occasionally, for 6–7 minutes until softened and lightly browned. Add the ginger, red chillies, tomatoes and lime leaves and cook for 2–3 minutes, stirring frequently. Return the aubergines to the pan with a splash of water and simmer gently for 2–3 minutes.

Remove from the heat and stir in the kecap manis, soy sauce, sugar, lime juice and chopped coriander.

Spoon into warm bowls, sprinkle over the chopped peanuts and serve with steamed noodles or rice.

For aubergine, tomato & chilli salad, drain 400 g (13 oz) chargrilled aubergines in olive oil from a jar, reserving the oil, and put the aubergines in a salad bowl with 8 sliced plum tomatoes and a handful of rocket leaves. Mix 6 tablespoons of the reserved oil, the juice of 2 lemons and 1 teaspoon chilli paste in a bowl, then season. Pour the dressing over the salad, toss to mix well and serve with crusty bread. **Total cooking time 10 minutes.**

tofu with pak choi & spring onions

Serves **4**
Total cooking time **20 minutes**

2 tablespoons **sunflower oil**
2 teaspoons grated **fresh root ginger**
8 **garlic cloves**, roughly chopped
4 **shallots**, finely chopped
2 **red chillies**, deseeded and chopped
8 cm (3 inch) length of **trimmed lemongrass stalk**, finely chopped
1 teaspoon **ground turmeric**
400 ml (14 fl oz) **can coconut milk**
200 ml (7 fl oz) **hot vegetable stock**
400 g (13 oz) **baby pak choi**, halved or quartered
200 g (7 oz) **mangetout**
400 g (14 oz) **firm tofu**, cubed
1 tablespoon **dark soy sauce**
1 tablespoon **lime juice**
6 **spring onions**, thinly sliced
salt and **pepper**

To garnish
small handful of **Thai basil leaves**
sliced **red chillies**

Put the oil, ginger, garlic, shallots, red chillies, lemongrass, turmeric and half the coconut milk in a food processor or blender and blend until fairly smooth.

Heat a large nonstick wok or frying pan until hot, add the coconut milk mixture and stir-fry over a high heat for 3–4 minutes. Add the remaining coconut milk and the stock and bring to the boil, then reduce the heat to low and simmer gently, uncovered, for 6–8 minutes.

Add the pak choi, mangetout and tofu and simmer for a further 6–7 minutes. Stir in the soy sauce and lime juice, then season to taste and simmer for another 1–2 minutes.

Remove from the heat and stir in the spring onions. Ladle into warm bowls and serve scattered with Thai basil leaves and sliced red chillies.

For Japanese-style tofu with spring onions, cut 800 g (1¾ lb) firm tofu into cubes and place in a dish. Mix together 1 tablespoon sesame oil, 2 tablespoons sunflower oil, 1 tablespoon mirin, 4 tablespoons light soy sauce, 1 deseeded and diced red chilli and 1 teaspoon chilli powder mixed with 1 teaspoon sesame seeds and drizzle over the tofu. Sprinkle over 8 thinly sliced spring onions and serve. **Total cooking time 10 minutes.**

chilli & courgette penne

Serves **4**
Total cooking time **20 minutes**

1 tablespoon **butter**
1 tablespoon **olive oil**
2 **red chillies**, finely chopped
2 **garlic cloves**, finely chopped
4 **spring onions**, very finely
   chopped
3 **courgettes**, coarsely grated
finely grated rind of **1 lime**
150 g (5 oz) **cream cheese**
350 g (11½ oz) **dried**
   pennette or other **short-**
   shaped pasta
small handful of **flat leaf**
   parsley, chopped
salt and **pepper**

Heat the butter and oil in a large frying pan, add the red chillies, garlic, spring onions and courgettes and cook over a medium-low heat for 10 minutes or until softened.

Reduce the heat to low, add the lime rind and gently cook for 3–4 minutes, then add the cream cheese and mix together until the cheese melts. Season to taste.

Meanwhile, cook the pasta in a large saucepan of lightly salted boiling water according to the pack instructions until 'al dente'.

Drain the pasta and stir into the courgette mixture with the parsley. Spoon into warm bowls and serve.

For chilli & courgette stir-fry noodles, heat

2 tablespoons olive oil in a large frying pan, add 6 sliced spring onions, 2 crushed garlic cloves, 1 chopped red chilli and 2 coarsely grated courgettes and cook over a high heat for 4–5 minutes until softened, then add 600 g (1 lb 5 oz) fresh egg noodles and 4 tablespoons light soy sauce and toss to mix well. Stir-fry for 1–2 minutes or until piping hot. Serve immediately. **Total cooking time 10 minutes.**

thai massaman pumpkin curry

Serves **4**
Total cooking time **20 minutes**

2 tablespoons **vegetable oil**
2 tablespoons **Thai
massaman curry paste**
6 **shallots**, thinly sliced
8 cm (3 inch) length of
trimmed lemongrass stalk,
finely chopped
6 **green cardamom pods**
2 teaspoons **black mustard
seeds**
800 g (1¾ lb) **pumpkin flesh,**
peeled, deseeded and cut
into 1 cm (½ inch) cubes
200 ml (7 fl oz) **hot vegetable
stock**
400 ml (14 fl oz) **can coconut
milk**
juice of **1 lime**

To garnish
small handful of **Thai basil
leaves** or **mint leaves**
red chilli slivers

To serve (optional)
lime wedges
steamed jasmine rice

Heat the oil in a heavy-based saucepan, add the curry paste, shallots, lemongrass, cardamom and mustard seeds and fry over a medium heat for 1–2 minutes until fragrant.

Add the peeled and deseeded pumpkin and pour over the stock and coconut milk. Bring to a simmer, then cook for 10–12 minutes or until the pumpkin is tender.

Remove from the heat and stir in the lime juice. Ladle into warm bowls, scatter with Thai basil or mint leaves and red chilli slivers. Serve with lime wedges for squeezing over and steamed jasmine rice, if liked.

For spicy roast Thai massaman vegetables, cut 500 g (1 lb) peeled and deseeded pumpkin, 2 cored and deseeded red peppers and 1 large aubergine into 2 cm (¾ inch) cubes and place in an ovenproof dish. Mix together 2 tablespoons Thai massaman curry paste and 200 ml (7 fl oz) canned coconut milk in a bowl. Pour the mixture over the vegetables, toss to mix well and season with salt. Place in a preheated oven, 200°C (400°F), Gas Mark 6, for 20–25 minutes or until tender. Scatter with a small handful of Thai basil or mint leaves and serve with steamed rice. **Total cooking time 30 minutes.**

cumin potatoes with pomegranate

Serves **4**
Total cooking time **10 minutes**

½ **large pomegranate**
4 tablespoons **sunflower oil**
1–2 teaspoons **black mustard
  seeds**
1 teaspoon **hot chilli powder**
4 teaspoons **cumin seeds**
2 teaspoons **sesame seeds**
8–10 fresh **curry leaves**
  (optional)
2 teaspoons **ground cumin**
2 teaspoons **ground
  coriander**
1 teaspoon **ground turmeric**
500 g (1 lb) **cooked potatoes**,
  cut into 2.5 cm (1 inch) cubes
6 tablespoons chopped **fresh
  coriander leaves**
juice of 1 small **lemon**
salt and **pepper**

To remove the pomegranate seeds, place the pomegranate over a bowl, cut-side down, and hit with the back of a spoon, catching the seeds in the bowl. Set aside.

Heat the oil in a large wok or frying pan until hot, add the mustard seeds and cook over a medium-high heat for a few minutes until the seeds begin to pop. Add the chilli powder, cumin seeds, sesame seeds and curry leaves, if using, and stir-fry for 30 seconds until fragrant.

Add the ground spices and potatoes, season well, then increase the heat to high and stir-fry briskly for 4–5 minutes.

Remove from the heat and stir in the chopped coriander and pomegranate seeds. Stir in the lemon juice, then spoon into a warm serving dish and serve hot.

For roast cumin potato wedges, cut 1 kg (2¼ lb) large baking potatoes into wedges and cook in a saucepan of boiling water for 6–8 minutes. Drain well, then place in a large bowl. Mix together 3 teaspoons cumin seeds, 1 teaspoon black mustard seeds, 2 teaspoons crushed coriander seeds, 1 tablespoon hot curry powder and 6 tablespoons sunflower oil, season with sea salt, then drizzle over the potatoes. Toss to mix well. Spread the potatoes in a single layer on a nonstick baking sheet and place in a preheated oven, 220°C (425°F), Gas Mark 7, for 20–25 minutes. **Total cooking time 30 minutes.**

puy lentil & butter bean salad

Serves **4**
Total cooking time **10 minutes**

400 g (13 oz) **can Puy lentils**,
   rinsed and drained
400 g (13 oz) **can butter
   beans**, rinsed and drained
1 **red onion**, finely sliced
200 g (7 oz) **cherry tomatoes**,
   halved
50 g (2 oz) **flat leaf parsley**,
   roughly chopped

Dressing
6 tablespoons **extra-virgin
   olive oil**
2 **red chillies**, very finely diced
2 tablespoons **red wine
   vinegar**
1 teaspoon **Dijon** or
   wholegrain mustard
1 teaspoon **clear honey**
½ **garlic clove**, crushed

Put the lentils and butter beans in a large serving bowl,
then add the onion, cherry tomatoes and parsley.

Mix together all the dressing ingredients in a small bowl,
then pour over the salad, toss to mix well and serve.

For chillied Puy lentil & butter bean pasta, cook
250 g (11½ oz) orzo pasta in a large saucepan of
lightly salted boiling water according to the pack
instructions until just 'al dente', then drain and return
to the pan. Cover and keep warm. Heat 2 tablespoons
sunflower oil in a large frying pan, add 1 sliced red
onion, 2 sliced red chillies and 2 sliced garlic cloves
and cook over a medium heat, stirring occasionally, for
5–6 minutes until softened. Stir in a rinsed and drained
400 g (12 oz) can Puy lentils, a rinsed and drained
400 g (12 oz) can butter beans, 175 ml (6 fl oz) hot
vegetable stock and the cooked orzo and bring to the
boil, then reduce the heat to medium, cover and cook
for 5–6 minutes, stirring occasionally. Season, then
stir in a small handful of chopped flat leaf parsley
and serve. **Total cooking time 30 minutes.**

vegetable tempura with chilli sauce

Serves **4**

Total cooking time **20 minutes**

vegetable oil, for deep-frying
1 **large red pepper**, cored,
deseeded and cut into
chunks
150 g (5 oz) **baby corn**
150 g (5 oz) **broccoli florets**
100 g (3½ oz) **asparagus**
spears, trimmed
6 large **spring onions**, cut into
5 cm (2 inch) lengths
sweet chilli dipping sauce,
to serve

Batter
25 g (1 oz) **plain flour**
50 g (2 oz) **cornflour**
2 **eggs**, beaten
75 ml (3 fl oz) **beer**
salt

Make the batter. Sift the flour and cornflour into a bowl and season with a little salt. Make a well in the centre, add the eggs and whisk a little, then gradually add the beer, pouring it in slowly and whisking continuously to make a smooth batter.

Half fill a deep saucepan with vegetable oil and heat to 190°C (375°F), or until a cube of bread browns in 30 seconds. Working quickly, dip the vegetable pieces, one by one, into the batter. Deep-fry in batches in the hot oil for 1–2 minutes until lightly golden.

Remove with a slotted spoon, drain on kitchen paper and keep warm. Serve with sweet chilli dipping sauce.

For sweet chilli & tempura vegetable noodles, cook the Vegetable Tempura as above. Meanwhile, cook 200 g (7 oz) soba noodles and 150 g (5 oz) trimmed fine green beans in a saucepan of lightly salted boiling water for 10 minutes until tender. Drain well. In a large wok, toss the tempura with the noodles and beans. Mix together 125 ml (4 fl oz) sweet chilli sauce, 3 tablespoons soy sauce and 3 tablespoons sesame oil in a small bowl, then toss into the noodles. Serve hot. **Total cooking time 30 minutes.**

spinach, tomato & paneer curry

Serves **4**

Total cooking time **30 minutes**

500 g (1 lb) **spinach leaves**

3 tablespoons **butter**

2 teaspoons **cumin seeds**

1 **red chilli**, deseeded and finely chopped

1 **onion**, very finely chopped

2 **plum tomatoes**, finely chopped

2 teaspoons finely grated **garlic**

1 tablespoon peeled and finely grated **fresh root ginger**

1 teaspoon **chilli powder**

1 teaspoon **ground coriander**

250 g (8 oz) **paneer** (**Indian cottage cheese**), cut into bite-sized pieces

2 tablespoons **double cream**

1 teaspoon **lemon juice**

2 tablespoons finely chopped **fresh coriander leaves**

salt and **pepper**

flatbreads, to serve (optional)

Cook the spinach in a large saucepan of boiling water for 2–3 minutes, then drain well. Transfer to a food processor or blender and blend to a smooth purée.

Heat the butter in a large wok or frying pan, add the cumin seeds, red chilli and onion and stir-fry over a medium-low heat for 6–8 minutes until the onions have softened. Add the tomatoes, garlic, ginger, chilli powder and ground coriander and season well. Stir through and cook for 2–3 minutes.

Increase the heat to high, add the paneer and stir-fry for 1–2 minutes, then add the spinach purée and stir-fry for a further 4–5 minutes until well mixed and heated through.

Remove from the heat and stir in the cream, lemon juice and chopped coriander. Spoon into warm bowls and serve with warm flatbreads, if liked.

For spicy spinach, tomato & cottage cheese salad, put 80 g (3 oz) baby spinach leaves and 400 g (13 oz) halved cherry tomatoes in a salad bowl. Mix together 400 g (13 oz) natural cottage cheese, 1 teaspoon ginger paste, 1 teaspoon garlic paste, 1 teaspoon chilli paste and 2 teaspoons toasted cumin seeds in a bowl, then season. Add to the spinach and tomatoes, toss gently to mix and serve with crusty bread or warm baguettes. **Total cooking time 10 minutes.**

spiced okra, tomato & coconut

Serves **4**
Total cooking time **20 minutes**

2 tablespoons **sunflower oil**
6–8 fresh **curry leaves**
2 teaspoons **black mustard
seeds**
1 **onion**, finely chopped
2 teaspoons **ground cumin**
1 teaspoon **ground coriander**
2 teaspoons **medium** or **hot
curry powder**
1 teaspoon **ground turmeric**
3 **garlic cloves**, finely chopped
500 g (1 lb) **okra**, trimmed
and cut diagonally into
2.5 cm (1 inch) pieces
2 **ripe plum tomatoes**,
chopped
3 tablespoons grated **fresh
coconut**, to garnish
salt and **pepper**

Heat the oil in a large wok or frying pan until hot, add the curry leaves, mustard seeds and onion and stir-fry over a medium heat for 3–4 minutes until fragrant and the onion is beginning to soften. Add the cumin, ground coriander, curry powder and turmeric and stir-fry for a further 30 seconds until fragrant.

Add the garlic and okra, increase the heat to high and stir-fry for 2–3 minutes, then add the tomatoes and season well. Cover, then reduce the heat to low and cook gently, stirring occasionally, for 10–12 minutes or until the okra is just tender.

Remove from the heat and sprinkle over the coconut, then ladle into warm bowls and serve.

For tomato, coconut & okra curry, heat 2 tablespoons sunflower oil in a large saucepan, add 1 chopped onion and cook over a medium heat, stirring occasionally, for 4–5 minutes until softened. Stir in a 400 g (13 oz) can chopped tomatoes and 2 tablespoons medium or hot curry powder, increase the heat to high and cook for 4–5 minutes, then add a 400 ml (14 fl oz) can coconut milk and bring back to the boil. Add 500 g (1 lb) okra, trimmed and cut into 2 cm (¾ inch) pieces, then reduce the heat to medium, cover and simmer gently for 10–12 minutes or until the okra is just tender. Season well. Serve with steamed rice and warm naan breads. **Total cooking time 30 minutes.**

spicy tabbouleh with roasted veg

Serves **4**
Total cooking time **30 minutes**

1 **courgette**, cut into bite-sized
  pieces
2 **red peppers**, cored,
  deseeded and cut into
  bite-sized pieces
1 **yellow pepper**, cored,
  deseeded and cut into bite-
  sized pieces
4 tablespoons **olive oil**
3 **garlic cloves**, crushed
1 **red chilli**, finely chopped
2 tablespoons **harissa paste**
125 g (4 oz) **bulgar wheat**
600 ml (1 pint) **hot vegetable
stock**
juice of **1 lemon**
6 tablespoons finely chopped
  fresh coriander leaves
6 tablespoons finely chopped
  mint leaves

Put the courgettes and peppers in a roasting tin. Mix together the oil, garlic, red chilli and harissa in a bowl, then pour over the vegetables and toss to coat evenly. Place in a preheated oven, 200°C (400°F), Gas Mark 6, for 20 minutes or until softened and the vegetables are just beginning to char at the edges.

Meanwhile, put the bulgar wheat in a large heatproof bowl and pour over the stock, then cover tightly with cling film and leave to stand for 15 minutes until the grains are tender but still have a little bite.

Leave the bulgar wheat to cool slightly, then add the roasted vegetables, lemon juice and chopped herbs and toss to mix well. Serve warm or at room temperature.

For Moroccan vegetable couscous salad, put 500 g (1 lb) shop-bought fresh Moroccan-style couscous salad in a large bowl with a 100 g (2½ oz) bag mixed salad leaves, 2 drained 270 g (9 oz) jars chargrilled peppers in olive oil and a small handful each of chopped coriander and mint leaves. Season, then toss to mix well and serve. **Total cooking time 10 minutes.**

thai vegetable curry

Serves **4**
Total cooking time **20 minutes**

500 g (1 lb) **butternut
  squash**, peeled, deseeded
  and cut into chunks
2 **red peppers**, cored,
  deseeded and cut into
  chunks
175 g (6 oz) **baby corn**, halved
250 g (8 oz) **cauliflower
  florets**
2 tablespoons **Thai green
  curry paste**
2 x 400 g (13 oz) **cans
  coconut milk**
150 ml (¼ pint) **vegetable
  stock**
175 g (6 oz) **sugar snap peas**
2 tablespoons **cold water**
1 tablespoon **cornflour**
4 tablespoons chopped **fresh
  coriander**
Thai jasmine rice, to serve
  (optional)

Place the squash, red peppers, corn and cauliflower
in a large, heavy-based saucepan, add the curry paste,
coconut milk and stock and bring to the boil. Reduce
the heat, cover with a lid and simmer for 15 minutes
until the vegetables are tender, adding the sugar snap
peas for the final 5 minutes of cooking.

Blend the measured water with the cornflour, add to
the curry and cook, stirring constantly, until it thickens
slightly. Stir in the coriander and serve with Thai Jasmine
rice, if liked.

For Thai corn & cauliflower curried soup, dice
250 g (8 oz) cauliflower florets and place in a large,
heavy-based saucepan with 2 x 400 g (13 oz) cans
coconut milk, 2 tablespoons Thai green curry paste,
150 ml (¼ pint) vegetable stock and 175 g (6 oz)
halved baby corn. Cook, stirring occasionally, for
9 minutes over a high heat. Stir in 4 tablespoons
chopped fresh coriander before serving. **Total
cooking time 10 minutes.**

spicy kidney beans with rice

Serves **4**
Total cooking time **20 minutes**

250 g (8 oz) **long-grain rice**
2 tablespoons **olive** or **vegetable oil**
1 **large red onion**, chopped
1 **red pepper**, cored, deseeded and chopped
2 **celery sticks**, chopped
2 teaspoons **Cajun-** or **Mexican-style spice blend**
2 x 400 g (13 oz) **cans red kidney beans**, drained and rinsed
3 **ripe tomatoes**, diced
1 tablespoon **red wine vinegar**
1 teaspoon **Tabasco sauce**, plus extra to serve
125 ml (4 fl oz) **water**
salt and **pepper**
2 tablespoons **chopped chives**, to garnish (optional)
4 tablespoons **crème fraîche**, to serve (optional)

Bring a large pan of lightly salted water to the boil and cook the rice for 12 minutes, or according to pack instructions, until just tender. Drain and keep hot.

Meanwhile, heat the oil in a large, deep-sided frying pan and add the onion, pepper and celery. Cook for 8–9 minutes, until softened. Add the spice mix, cook for 1 minute, then stir in the kidney beans, tomatoes, vinegar, Tabasco and measured water.

Cover and simmer gently for 7–8 minutes, adding a little more water if necessary. Season to taste and scatter with the chopped chives, if using. Serve with the tender rice, extra Tabasco and crème fraîche, if liked.

For spicy Mexican rice salad, deseed and finely chop 1 red pepper and mix with ½ a finely chopped red onion and 2 finely chopped celery sticks. Stir in 250 g (8 oz) cooked wild and basmati rice and a 400 g (13 oz) can of kidney beans, rinsed and drained. Add 2 deseeded and chopped tomatoes, 2 tablespoons chopped chives and 2 tablespoons lime juice. Season generously and serve with lightly salted tortilla chips. **Total cooking time 10 minutes.**

marinated tofu with vegetables

Serves **4**

Total cooking time **30 minutes**

3 tablespoons **ketjap manis**
   or **sweet soy sauce**

1 teaspoon crushed **garlic**

2 teaspoons minced **fresh
   root ginger**

2 tablespoons **sweet chilli
   dipping sauce**

500 g (1 lb) **firm tofu**, cut into
   1.5 cm (¾ inch) slices

2 tablespoons **vegetable** or
   groundnut oil

1 **carrot**, peeled and cut into
   fine matchsticks

500 g (1 lb) **pak choi**, sliced

200 g (7 oz) **beansprouts**

225 g (7½ oz) **can bamboo
   shoots in water**

6 tablespoons **oyster sauce**

2 teaspoons **golden sesame
   seeds**, to garnish (optional)

Mix the ketjap manis, garlic, ginger and sweet chilli dipping sauce in a small bowl. Arrange the tofu slices in a shallow dish and pour over the marinade, turning to coat. Set aside to marinate for about 20 minutes.

Transfer the tofu slices to a foil-lined grill rack, reserving the marinade. Cook under a preheated hot grill for about 3 minutes on each side, until golden. Remove from the heat and keep warm.

Meanwhile, heat the oil in a wok over a moderate heat. Stir-fry the carrot and pak choi for 4–5 minutes, until beginning to soften. Add the beansprouts and bamboo shoots and cook for 1 minute, then pour in the remaining marinade and the oyster sauce.

Spoon the vegetables into deep bowls, top with the grilled tofu slices and sprinkle with golden sesame seeds, if using.

For tofu & vegetable noodles, cook the stir-fried vegetables following the recipe above, adding 150 g (5 oz) ready-prepared marinated tofu strips or cubed firm tofu, along with the beansprouts and bamboo shoots. Meanwhile, cook 250 g (8 oz) medium dried egg noodles according to the pack instructions, then drain and toss with the vegetables and tofu. Serve with soy sauce. **Total cooking time 20 minutes.**

spicy chickpea curry

Serves **4**
Total cooking time **30 minutes**

2 tablespoons **sunflower oil**
4 **garlic cloves**, crushed
2 teaspoons peeled and finely
grated **fresh root ginger**
1 large **onion**, coarsely grated
1–2 **green chillies**, finely
sliced
1 teaspoon **hot chilli powder**
1 tablespoon **ground cumin**
1 tablespoon **ground**
coriander
3 tablespoons **natural yogurt**,
plus extra, whisked, to serve
2 teaspoons **garam masala**
500 ml (17 fl oz) **water**
2 teaspoons **tamarind paste**
2 teaspoons **medium** or **hot**
curry powder
2 x 400 g (13 oz) **cans**
chickpeas, rinsed and
drained
chopped **fresh coriander**
leaves, to garnish
lemon wedges, to serve
(optional)

Heat the oil in a large heavy-based frying pan, add the garlic, ginger, onion and green chillies and cook over a medium heat, stirring occasionally, for 5–6 minutes until the onion is lightly golden. Add the chilli powder, cumin, ground coriander, yogurt and garam masala and cook for a further 1–2 minutes.

Stir in the measured water and bring to the boil. Add the tamarind paste, curry powder and chickpeas and bring back to the boil, then reduce the heat to medium and cook, uncovered, for 15–20 minutes or until the sauce is thickened.

Ladle into warm bowls, drizzle with extra whisked yogurt and scatter with chopped coriander. Serve with lemon wedges for squeezing over, if liked.

For spicy chickpea soup, heat 2 tablespoons sunflower oil in a saucepan, add 1 chopped onion and cook, stirring, for 1–2 minutes until softened. Add 1 tablespoon medium or hot curry powder and 600 ml (1 pint) hot vegetable stock and bring to the boil, then add a rinsed and drained 400 g (12 oz) can chickpeas and 200 ml (7 fl oz) single cream. Bring back to the boil, then reduce the heat to medium and cook for 4–5 minutes or until piping hot. Season, stir in 4 tablespoons chopped coriander leaves and serve with crusty bread. **Total cooking time 20 minutes.**

spiced broad bean & dill pilau

Serves **4**
Total cooking time **30 minutes**

300 g (10 oz) podded **broad beans**
50 g (2 oz) **butter**
2 **red chillies**, finely chopped
1 tablespoon **cumin seeds**
2 **whole cloves**
6 **green cardamom pods**
1 **cinnamon stick**
50 g (2 oz) **red split lentils**, rinsed and drained
250 g (8 oz) **basmati rice**
6 **spring onions**, finely sliced
6 tablespoons finely chopped **dill**
salt and **pepper**

Cook the broad beans in a saucepan of boiling water for 1–2 minutes. Drain, then put in a bowl of cold water and leave the beans to cool slightly. Drain again, then slip off and discard the skins and set the beans aside.

Melt the butter in a saucepan over a low heat, add the red chillies and spices and stir for 1 minute, then add the lentils and rice and continue to stir until well coated.

Pour over enough water to come about 1.5 cm (¾ inch) above the level of the rice. Season well and bring to the boil. Stir once, then reduce the heat to very low, cover tightly and cook gently for 8–10 minutes. Remove from the heat and leave to stand, covered, for 10–12 minutes or until the liquid is absorbed and the rice is tender.

Stir the broad beans, spring onions and dill through the rice, then spoon into a bowls and serve.

For spicy broad bean & dill rice salad, blanch and skin 400 g (12 oz) podded broad beans as above. Meanwhile, heat a frying pan until hot, add 1 tablespoon cumin seeds and dry-fry over a medium heat until browned, then leave to cool. Put 500 g (1 lb) shop-bought fresh boiled rice, 2 finely chopped red chillies, the toasted cumin seeds, 6 finely sliced spring onions and the broad beans in a large bowl. Pour 150 ml (¼ pint) shop-bought fresh vinaigrette over the salad and scatter with a small handful of chopped dill. Season, toss to mix well and serve.
Total cooking time 10 minutes.

carrot, pea & potato curry

Serves **4**
Total cooking time **30 minutes**

2 teaspoons **vegetable oil**
3 **whole cloves**
2 **cinnamon sticks**
2 teaspoons **white poppy seeds**
2 teaspoons **black peppercorns**
4 **dried red chillies**
75 g (3 oz) **unsweetened desiccated coconut**, lightly toasted
4 **garlic cloves**, roughly chopped
2 **onions**, roughly chopped
4 teaspoons **sunflower oil**
2 **potatoes**, peeled and chopped into 2.5 cm (1 inch) cubes
2 **large carrots**, peeled and chopped into 2.5 cm (1 inch) cubes
400 g (13 oz) **can chopped tomatoes**
200 g (7 oz) **frozen peas**
salt
mini naan breads, to serve

To make the spice paste, heat the vegetable oil in a small frying pan over a medium heat, add the cloves, cinnamon sticks, poppy seeds, peppercorns and dried chillies and fry for 1–2 minutes until fragrant. Put in a food processor or blender with the coconut, garlic and onions and blitz to a coarse paste.

Heat the sunflower oil in a heavy-based saucepan, add the potatoes and carrots, then cover and cook over a medium heat for 2 minutes. Stir in the spice paste and chopped tomatoes and season with salt.

Stir, re-cover and simmer for 15–20 minutes or until the potatoes and carrots are tender, adding the peas 5 minutes before the end of the cooking time.

Spoon into warm bowls and serve with mini naan breads.

For spicy pea, carrot & potato stir-fry, heat 2 tablespoons olive oil in a large wok until hot, add 2 teaspoons black mustard seeds and cook over a high heat until the seeds begin to pop. Add 2 teaspoons cumin seeds, 1 teaspoon ground cumin, 1 teaspoon ground coriander, 2 teaspoons hot chilli powder, a drained 300 g (10 oz) can new potatoes, diced, a drained 300 g (10 oz) can baby carrots, diced and 300 g (10 oz) frozen peas. Stir-fry over a high heat for 4–5 minutes. Remove from the heat, squeeze over the juice of 1 lemon and serve. **Total cooking time 10 minutes.**

curried mushrooms & tomatoes

Serves **4**
Total cooking time **20 minutes**

5 tablespoons **sunflower oil**
500 g (1 lb) **chestnut mushrooms**, halved or thickly sliced
100 ml (3½ fl oz) **double cream**
2 **ripe plum tomatoes**, finely chopped
6 tablespoons finely chopped **fresh coriander leaves**
salt and **pepper**
steamed rice, to serve

Spice paste
4 **garlic cloves**, finely chopped
2 teaspoons peeled and finely chopped **fresh root ginger**
1 **onion**, finely chopped
1 tablespoon **medium** or **hot curry powder**
3 tablespoons **water**

Make the spice paste. Put all the ingredients in a food processor or blender and blend until smooth.

Heat 3 tablespoons of the oil in a large wok until hot, add the mushrooms and stir-fry over a high heat for 4–5 minutes. Transfer the contents of the wok to a bowl and wipe out the wok with kitchen paper.

Heat the remaining oil in the wok until hot, add the curry paste and stir-fry over a medium heat for 3–4 minutes. Return the mushrooms and any juices to the wok, add the cream and tomatoes and cook, stirring, for 3–4 minutes or until piping hot. Season well.

Remove from the heat, stir in the chopped coriander and serve immediately with steamed rice.

For spicy mushroom & tomato stir-fry, heat 2 tablespoons sunflower oil in a large wok or frying pan until hot, add 500 g (1 lb) large sliced chestnut mushrooms, 1 tablespoon medium or hot curry powder, 1 teaspoon ginger paste and 1 teaspoon garlic paste and stir-fry over a high heat for 4–5 minutes. Stir in 100 ml (3½ fl oz) double cream and 2 chopped tomatoes and cook for 2–3 minutes or until piping hot. Scatter with a small handful of chopped coriander and serve with steamed rice or noodles. **Total cooking time 10 minutes.**

food for friends

asparagus carbonara

Serves **4**

Total cooking time **10 minutes**

1 tablespoon **olive oil**

2 **spring onions**, chopped

150 g (5 oz) **fine asparagus spears**

pinch of chopped **tarragon**

500 g (1 lb) **fresh linguine**

1 **egg**, lightly beaten

50 g (2 oz) **crème fraîche**

50 g (2 oz) **Italian-style hard cheese**, grated, plus extra to serve

salt and **pepper**

Heat the oil in a large frying pan. Add the spring onions and asparagus and cook for 2–3 minutes until just cooked through. Stir in the tarragon.

Cook the linguine in a large saucepan of lightly salted boiling water according to the pack instructions. Drain, reserving a little cooking water, and return to the pan. Add the cooked asparagus and spring onions, then add the egg, crème fraîche and Italian-style hard cheese . Season and stir together until creamy, adding a little of the pasta cooking water if needed. Spoon into bowls and scatter over more cheese to serve.

For poached eggs with asparagus, toss 150 g (5 oz) asparagus spears in 2 tablespoons olive oil. Cook on a hot griddle pan for 5 minutes, turning frequently, until charred and cooked through. Whisk together 2 tablespoons lemon juice, 4 tablespoons olive oil, add 1 crushed garlic clove and season. Cut ¼ baguette into small chunks, toss with 5 tablespoons olive oil and bake in a preheated oven, 200°C (400°F), Gas Mark 6, for 7–10 minutes until golden, then leave to cool. Poach 4 eggs for 4 minutes for a soft yolk, then pat dry with kitchen paper. Toss the lemon dressing with 150 g (5 oz) spinach leaves and the asparagus. Arrange on plates with the eggs, croûtons and shavings of Italian-style hard cheese. **Total cooking time 20 minutes.**

jewelled fruity spicy pilaf

Serves **4**

Total cooking time **30 minutes**

1 tablespoon **saffron threads**
1 litre (1¾ pints) **hot vegetable stock**
400 g (13 oz) **basmati rice**
1 tablespoon **olive oil**
1 tablespoon **butter**
3 **shallots**, finely chopped
2 **garlic cloves**, finely chopped
4 **cardamom pods**, lightly bruised
2 **whole cloves**
2 **cinnamon sticks**
2 teaspoons **cumin seeds**
2 **carrots**, peeled and finely diced
4 tablespoons chopped **dill**
300 g (10 oz) podded **soya beans**
100 g (3½ oz) **golden sultanas**
100 g (3½ oz) **dried cranberries**
seeds from 1 **ripe pomegranate**
50 g (2 oz) **slivered pistachio nuts**
salt and pepper

Add the saffron to the hot stock and set aside.

Rinse the rice in cold running water and leave to drain.

Heat the oil and butter in a heavy-based saucepan and stir-fry the shallots and garlic for 1–2 minutes over a medium heat.

Add the cardamom pods, cloves, cinnamon sticks, cumin seeds, rice and carrots and stir to mix well. Add the stock mixture along with the dill, season and bring up to the boil. Stir in the soya beans, golden sultanas and dried cranberries. Cover tightly and reduce the heat to low. Cook for 10–12 minutes without lifting the lid.

Remove from the heat and allow to stand, undisturbed, for 10 minutes.

Remove the lid (the liquid should have been completely absorbed), stir in the pomegranate seeds and pistachio nuts and serve immediately.

For fruity spiced couscous, place 400 g (13 oz) cooked couscous in a wide bowl with 1 finely julienned carrot, 2 finely sliced shallots, 100 g (3½ oz) golden sultanas, 100 g (3½ oz) chopped dill and 100 g (3½ oz) pomegranate seeds. Whisk together 6 tablespoons olive oil with the juice of 1 orange, 1 teaspoon each of ground cinnamon and cumin and pour over the couscous mixture. Season, toss to mix well and serve. **Total cooking time 10 minutes.**

beetroot & goats' cheese tarte tatin

Serves **4–6**
Total cooking time **30 minutes**

2 tablespoons **olive oil**
2 **garlic cloves**, chopped
1 teaspoon **thyme leaves**
2 tablespoons **balsamic vinegar**
500 g (1 lb) **cooked beetroot** (not pickled), sliced or cut into thin wedges
flour, for dusting
250 g (8 oz) **shop-bought chilled puff pastry**
125 g (4 oz) **crumbly goats' cheese**
thyme leaves or **snipped chives**, to garnish

Place the oil in an ovenproof frying pan over a medium-low heat and, when hot, fry the garlic and thyme for 1–2 minutes, until just softened. Pour in the vinegar and simmer gently for 1–2 minutes, until just sticky.

Arrange the beetroot to fit snugly and attractively in the pan, then increase the heat slightly and cook for 4–5 minutes, until the underside begins to brown.

Meanwhile, place the pastry on a lightly floured work surface and roll into a circle about 1 cm (½ inch) larger than the pan.

Lay the pastry over the pan, tucking the edges in neatly to cover the beetroot, and bake in a preheated oven, 200°C (400°F), Gas Mark 6, for 15–20 minutes, until the pastry is puffed and golden.

Invert the tarte onto a large plate, then crumble over the goats' cheese and serve garnished with the thyme or chives.

For individual goats' cheese & beetroot quiches,

unroll a 320 g (10¾ oz) sheet of chilled shortcrust pastry and use to line 4 greased, individual quiche tins. Fill the pastry cases with 175 g (6 oz) diced, cooked beetroot, 100 g (3½ oz) defrosted peas and 100 g (3½ oz) crumbled goats' cheese. Break 3 eggs into a jug, beat together, then mix in 3 tablespoons single cream and 1 teaspoon chopped thyme leaves. Pour into the filled cases and bake in a preheated oven, 220°C (425°F), Gas Mark 7, for 12–15 minutes, or until set and golden. **Total cooking time 20 minutes.**

mushroom risotto

Serves **4**

Total cooking time **30 minutes**

10 g (⅓ oz) **dried porcini**
200 ml (7 fl oz) **boiling water**
1 tablespoon **olive oil**
2 **shallots**, diced
350 g (11½ oz) **Arborio rice**
150 ml (¼ pint) **white wine**
600 ml (1 pint) **hot vegetable
stock**
175 g (6 oz) **chestnut
mushrooms**
1 teaspoon chopped **thyme
leaves**
salt and **pepper**
2 tablespoons grated **Italian-
style hard cheese**, to serve

Place the dried porcini in a bowl and cover with the measured water. Leave to stand for 15 minutes.

Meanwhile, heat the olive oil in a saucepan and sauté the shallots for 2–3 minutes, unitl softened but not coloured.

Stir in the rice and continue to stir, until the edges of the grains look translucent.

Pour in the wine, and cook for 1–2 minutes over a high heat and stir until it is absorbed.

Add a ladle of the hot stock, reduce the heat to medium, and stir continuously until it has been absorbed. Repeat with the remaining hot stock, a ladle at a time.

Drain the porcini, reserving the liquid. Roughly chop the porcini and add to the rice with the fresh mushrooms and a ladle of the porcini liquid.

Continue to stir and add liquid, until the rice is 'al dente'.

Stir in the thyme, season to taste and serve sprinkled with grated cheese.

For quick mushroom rice, heat 2 tablespoons olive oil in a frying pan and fry 350 g (11½ oz) chestnut mushrooms and 4 sliced spring onions for 5–6 minutes. Stir in a 400 g (13 oz) pack ready-cooked rice and 1 tablespoon chopped parsley. Season and serve sprinkled with 2 tablespoons grated Italian-style hard cheese. **Total cooking time 10 minutes.**

watercress, raisins & pine nut fusilli

Serves **4**

Total cooking time **10 minutes**

400 g (13 oz) **fusilli**
2 tablespoons **olive oil**
225 g (7½ oz) **watercress**,
  roughly chopped
50 g (2 oz) **raisins**
60 g (2¼ oz) **toasted pine
  nuts**
grated rind of 1 **lemon**
Italian-style hard cheese
  shavings, to serve

Cook the fusilli in a saucepan of boiling water according to the pack instructions, until 'al dente'.

Meanwhile, heat the olive oil in a large saucepan and add the watercress. Stir until wilted and then add the raisins.

Drain the pasta and add to the watercress and raisins. Add the pine nuts and lemon rind, then toss together.

Serve sprinkled with Italian-style hard cheese shavings.

For fusilli & watercress salad, cook 300 g (10 oz) fusilli in a saucepan of boiling water according to the pack instructions, until al dente. Drain and refresh under cold water. Mix the pasta together with 2 carrots, 2 courgettes and 1 cored and deseeded red pepper, which have all been cut into matchsticks. Add 75 g (3 oz) watercress. Whisk together 3 tablespoons extra-virgin olive oil, 1 tablespoon sherry vinegar, 1 crushed garlic clove, ½ teaspoon mustard and ½ teaspoon clear honey. Drizzle the dressing over the salad and serve sprinkled with 2 tablespoons toasted pine nuts. **Total cooking time 20 minutes.**

herby mushrooms with polenta

Serves **4**

Total cooking time **30 minutes**

150 g (5 oz) **polenta**

1 tablespoon finely chopped
rosemary leaves

1 tablespoon finely chopped
sage leaves

8 tablespoons finely chopped
flat leaf parsley

8 tablespoons **butter**

1.5 litres (2½ pints) **hot
vegetable stock**

750 g (1½ lb) **large
Portobello mushrooms,**
thickly sliced

3 **garlic cloves**, crushed

8 tablespoons **soft cheese
with garlic and herbs**

½ teaspoon **crushed dried
red chilli**

salt and **pepper**

Place the polenta, rosemary, sage, half the parsley and half the butter in a saucepan over a medium heat and gradually whisk in the stock, stirring continuously.

Reduce the heat to low, season well and stir constantly until the polenta becomes very thick and starts bubbling (this will take about 6–8 minutes). Remove from the heat and keep warm.

Meanwhile, heat the remaining butter in a large nonstick frying pan over a high heat. Add the mushrooms and garlic and stir-fry for 6–8 minutes. Season well and stir in the soft cheese and dried chilli. Stir-fry for 2–3 minutes until bubbling. Remove from the heat and stir in the remaining parsley.

Serve immediately on warmed plates over the polenta.

For creamy mushroom & herb pasta, cook 375 g (12 oz) quick-cook pasta according to the pack instructions. Meanwhile, heat a large frying pan over a high heat and add 2 tablespoons butter, 2 finely chopped garlic cloves and 750 g (1½ lb) thinly sliced Portobello mushrooms. Stir-fry over a high heat for 3–4 minutes, then stir in 200 g (7 oz) soft cheese with garlic and herbs. Season, toss to mix well and stir in 3 tablespoons chopped flat leaf parsley. Serve over the pasta. **Total cooking time 10 minutes.**

asparagus & fontina crespelles

Serves **4**

Total cooking time **30 minutes**

750 g (1 ½ lb) **asparagus**, woody ends trimmed

3 tablespoons **olive oil**

15 g (½ oz) **Italian-style hard cheese**, freshly grated, plus extra to sprinkle

500 g (1 lb) tub **ready-made white sauce**

freshly **grated nutmeg**, to taste

12 **ready-made savoury pancakes**

125 g (4 oz) **Fontina cheese**, grated, plus extra for sprinkling

Place the asparagus in a roasting tin, toss with the oil and roast in a preheated oven, 240°C (475°F), Gas Mark 9, for 7 minutes or until tender. Set aside.

Reduce the oven temperature to 220°C (425°F), Gas Mark 7.

Stir the Italian-style hard cheese into the white sauce and season with nutmeg. Spread a little sauce onto a pancake, top with asparagus and some Fontina. Roll up and place into a 2-litre (3½ -pint) ovenproof dish. Repeat with the remaining pancakes.

Drizzle the remaining sauce over the pancakes in the dish, sprinkle with the extra cheese and nutmeg. Bake for 12–15 minutes or until golden. Serve immediately.

For grilled asparagus bruschettas with melted fontina, blanch 625 g (1 ¼ lb) asparagus tips in a saucepan of lightly salted boiling water for 2–3 minutes. Drain and divide the asparagus between 8 slices of toasted sourdough bread and scatter over 200 g (7 oz) grated Fontina cheese. Grill under a preheated medium grill for 2–3 minutes or until the cheese has just melted. Season and serve with a crisp green salad. **Total cooking time 10 minutes.**

spicy tofu & mushroom stir-fry

Serves **4**

Total cooking time **10 minutes**

2 tablespoons **vegetable oil**
250 g (8 oz) **shiitake mushrooms**, halved if large
1 **leek** (white only), thinly sliced
2 **garlic cloves**, chopped
2 teaspoons grated **fresh root ginger**
3 tablespoons **black bean sauce**
1 teaspoon **chilli sauce**
pinch of **ground Sichuan pepper**
1 tablespoon **cornflour**
150 ml (¼ pint) **vegetable stock**
2 tablespoons **soy sauce**
1 tablespoon **rice wine vinegar**
1 tablespoon **caster sugar**
325 g (11 oz) **firm tofu**, cubed
2 **spring onions**, shredded
plain boiled rice, to serve

Heat the oil in a large wok, add the mushrooms and cook for 2 minutes. Add the leek and cook for 2 minutes until softened. Stir in the garlic and ginger, followed by the black bean and chilli sauces and the Sichuan pepper.

Mix together the cornflour, stock, soy sauce, vinegar and sugar and add to the wok. Carefully stir in the tofu. Leave to simmer for 2–3 minutes until the sauce has thickened. Sprinkle over the spring onions and serve with plain boiled rice.

For egg-fried tofu & shiitake rice, boil 250 g (8 oz) rice according to pack instructions, then drain. Heat 2 tablespoons oil in a wok, add 150 g (5 oz) cubed firm tofu and cook for 3 minutes. Remove from the wok. Add 150 g (5 oz) shiitake mushrooms. Cook for 2 minutes, then add 2 chopped garlic cloves, 1 teaspoon grated fresh root ginger and 2 chopped spring onions. Cook for 1 minute. Crack 1 egg into the wok and stir until just cooked. Add the rice, tofu, 50 g (2 oz) defrosted frozen peas and 3 tablespoons soy sauce, stir and serve. **Total cooking time 20 minutes.**

butternut risotto with chilli & ricotta

Serves **4**

Total cooking time **30 minutes**

50 g (2 oz) **butter**

1 tablespoon **olive oil**

1 **onion**, finely chopped

325 g (11 oz) **butternut squash**, peeled, deseeded and chopped

1 **red chilli**, deseeded and finely chopped

250 g (8 oz) **risotto rice**

100 ml (3½ fl oz) **dry white wine**

750 ml (1¼ pint) **hot vegetable stock**

50 g (2 oz) **Italian-style hard cheese**, grated

3 **sage leaves**, finely chopped

50 g (2 oz) **ricotta cheese**

salt and **pepper**

Heat half the butter with the oil in a large saucepan, add the onion and cook for 5 minutes until softened. Add the peeled and deseeded squash and cook for 2 minutes more. Stir most of the chilli into the pan along with the rice and cook for 2 minutes until the rice is well coated.

Pour the wine into the pan and cook until it has bubbled away. Gradually stir in the hot stock, a little at a time, stirring frequently and allowing the rice to absorb the stock before adding more. When the rice is soft, after about 15 minutes, stir in the remaining butter and the Italian-style hard cheese and season to taste. Spoon into serving bowls, sprinkle over the sage, ricotta and remaining chilli and serve.

For butternut chilli & ricotta gnocchi, cook

300 g (10 oz) peeled, deseeded and chopped butternut squash in a large saucepan of lightly salted boiling water for 3 minutes. Add 500 g (1 lb) fresh gnocchi and cook for 3 minutes or according to the pack instructions. Drain and toss through 2 finely chopped sage leaves, ½ teaspoon dried chilli flakes and 25 g (1 oz) butter. Season, then spoon onto serving plates and top with dollops of ricotta and some grated Italian-style hard cheese. **Total cooking time 10 minutes.**

puy lentil stew with garlic bread

Serves **4**
Total cooking time **30 minutes**

4 tablespoons **olive oil**
1 **red pepper**, cored,
    deseeded and cut into
    chunks
1 **green pepper**, cored,
    deseeded and cut into
    chunks
1 **red onion**, roughly chopped
1 **garlic clove**, sliced
1 **fennel bulb**, trimmed and
    sliced
250 g (8 oz) **Puy lentils**, rinsed
600 ml (1 pint) **vegetable
    stock**
300 ml (½ pint) **red wine**

Garlic bread
50 g (2 oz) **butter**, softened
1 **garlic clove**, crushed
2 tablespoons **thyme leaves**,
    roughly chopped
1 **wholemeal French
    baguette**
salt and **pepper**

Heat the oil in a large, heavy-based saucepan and cook the peppers, onion, garlic and fennel over a medium-high heat, stirring frequently, for 5 minutes until softened and lightly browned. Stir in the lentils, stock and wine and bring to the boil, then reduce the heat and simmer for 25 minutes until the lentils are tender.

Meanwhile, beat the softened butter with the garlic and thyme in a bowl and season with a little salt and pepper. Cut the baguette into thick slices, almost all the way through but leaving the base attached. Spread the butter thickly over each slice, then wrap the baguette in foil and place in a preheated oven, 200°C (400°F), Gas Mark 6, for 15 minutes.

Serve the stew hot, ladled into warm serving bowls, with the torn hot garlic and herb bread on the side for mopping up the juices.

For Puy lentil & sun-dried tomato salad, place 200 g (7 oz) rinsed Puy lentils in a saucepan, cover generously with cold water and bring to the boil. Reduce the heat and simmer for 15 minutes until just tender. Drain, then toss with the juice of 1 lemon, 1 crushed garlic clove and 4 tablespoons olive oil, and season with salt and pepper. Stir a drained 280 g (9¼ oz) jar sun-dried tomatoes, 1 small finely chopped red onion and a handful of chopped flat leaf parsley through the lentils and serve with some rocket leaves. **Total cooking time 20 minutes.**

herby tomato & cheese tart

Serves **4**
Total cooking time **30 minutes**

250 g (8 oz) chilled **puff pastry**

3–4 tablespoons **black olive tapenade** or **Dijon mustard**

300 g (10 oz) **ripe plum tomatoes**, finely sliced

8 large **basil leaves**, roughly torn

125 g (4 oz) **Camembert cheese**

100 g (3½ oz) **goats' cheese**

2 tablespoons **thyme leaves**, plus extra to garnish

1–2 tablespoons **extra virgin olive oil**

salt and **pepper**

Roll out the pastry and use it to line a 25 cm (10 inch) tart tin.

Spread the tapenade or Dijon mustard over the base of the tart.

Lay the tomato slices in concentric circles in the tart, discarding any juice or seeds that have run from them. Season the tomatoes (bearing in mind that tapenade is salty) and scatter over the basil.

Cut the Camembert and goats' cheese into thin wedges or slices, according to its shape. Arrange a circle of Camembert pieces around the outside and a circle of goats' cheese within. Put any remaining pieces of cheese in the middle.

Sprinkle over the thyme leaves and drizzle the olive oil on top.

Bake in a preheated oven, 200°C (400°F), Gas Mark 6, for 15–18 minutes until the pastry is cooked and the cheese is golden and bubbling. Serve immediately, garnished with thyme.

For fresh tomato & two cheese pasta, cook 375 g (12 oz) farfalle pasta according to the pack instructions. Meanwhile, finely chop 4 plum tomatoes, 100 g (3½ oz) pitted black olives, 25 g (1 oz) basil leaves and 2 tablespoons thyme leaves and place in a bowl with 100 g (3½ oz) each of diced goats' cheese and Camembert cheese. Drain the pasta and add to the tomato mixture. Season, toss to mix well and serve immediately. **Total cooking time 20 minutes.**

aubergine with cucumber noodles

Serves **4**
Total cooking time **20 minutes**

12 baby **aubergines**, halved
4 tablespoons **white miso paste**
3 tablespoons **rice wine vinegar**
2 tablespoons **caster sugar**
1 tablespoon **sake** or **water**
1 tablespoon **sesame seeds**
125 g (4 oz) **soy beans**
300 g (10 oz) **ready-cooked rice noodles**
½ **cucumber**, thinly sliced
2 **spring onions**, thinly sliced
salt

Make a criss-cross pattern on the cut sides of the aubergines and place them, cut side down, on a grill pan. Cook for 7–10 minutes under a preheated hot grill until charred. Mix together the miso paste, 2 tablespoons of the vinegar, the sugar and sake or water. Turn the aubergines over and brush with the miso mixture. Return to the grill for 3–5 minutes until the aubergine is soft, then sprinkle with the sesame seeds and cook for 1 minute more.

Meanwhile, cook the soy beans in a saucepan of lightly salted boiling water for 2 minutes until soft. Drain and cool under cold running water. Toss the beans together with the noodles, cucumber, spring onions, the remaining vinegar and season with salt. Serve with the grilled aubergine.

For grilled aubergine salad with miso ginger dressing, cut 2 large aubergines into thin slices and toss together with 6 tablespoons vegetable oil. Cook on a hot griddle pan for 2–3 minutes on each side until charred and soft. Mix together 1 tablespoon white miso paste with 2 tablespoons rice wine vinegar, a pinch of caster sugar, 2 teaspoons grated fresh root ginger and ½ finely chopped red chilli. Whisk in 5 tablespoons vegetable oil, then toss together with the grilled aubergine and 200 g (7 oz) rocket leaves. **Total cooking time 10 minutes.**

butter bean & vegetable crumble

Serves **4**

Total cooking time **30 minutes**

75 g (3 oz) **butter**, chilled
  and diced
175 g (6 oz) **plain flour**
100 g (3½ oz) **walnuts**,
  chopped
50 g (2 oz) **Cheddar cheese**,
  grated
2 x 250 g (8 oz) packs
  prepared **peas, cauliflower**
  and **carrots**
500 g (1 lb) **jar ready-made**
  tomato and herb sauce
2 **garlic cloves**, crushed
6 tablespoons finely chopped
  basil leaves
400 g (13 oz) **can butter**
  beans, drained and rinsed
salt and **pepper**

Rub the butter into the plain flour until crumbs form. Stir in the chopped walnuts and grated cheese, season and set aside.

Remove the carrots from the packs of prepared vegetables, roughly chop and boil for 2 minutes. Add the peas and cauliflower and cook for another minute, then drain.

Meanwhile, heat the tomato and herb sauce in a large saucepan until bubbling.

Stir in the garlic, basil, butter beans and blanched vegetables. Transfer to a medium-sized ovenproof dish and scatter over the crumble mixture. Bake in a preheated oven, 200°C (400°F), Gas Mark 6, for 15–20 minutes or until golden and bubbling.

For butter bean & walnut pâté, tip 2 x 400 g (13 oz) cans butter beans, rinsed and drained, and the juice and finely grated zest of 1 lemon into a blender or food processor with 1 crushed garlic clove, 4 tablespoons each of finely chopped basil and mint leaves, 50 g (2 oz) chopped walnuts, 8 tablespoons ready-made mayonnaise and 2 teaspoons Dijon mustard. Blend until fairly smooth and serve spread thickly on toasted sourdough bread with a salad. **Total cooking time 10 minutes.**

leek & blue cheese tart

Serves **4**

Total cooking time **30 minutes**

150 g (5 oz) **baby leeks**,
  trimmed

325 g (11 oz) chilled **ready-
  rolled puff pastry**

oil, for greasing

1 **egg**, beaten

75 g (3 oz) **mascarpone
  cheese**

125 g (4 oz) **blue cheese**

salt and **pepper**

Cook the leeks in a pan of lightly salted boiling water for 1 minute until just soft. Drain and cool under cold running water.

Unwrap the pastry onto a lightly greased baking sheet. Use a sharp knife to lightly score a 1 cm (½ inch) border all around the pastry, taking care not to cut all the way through. Lightly prick the inside of the pastry with the end of a fork and brush all over the border with egg.

Mix together the remaining egg, the mascarpone and half the blue cheese and spread the mixture over the pastry. Arrange the leeks on top and scatter over the remaining cheese. Cook in a preheated oven, 200°C (400°F), Gas Mark 6, for 20 minutes until the pastry is golden and cooked through.

For creamy leek & blue cheese pasta, cut 2 large leeks into thin slices. Cook in a large pan of lightly salted boiling water for 3–5 minutes until soft, together with 500 g (1 lb) fresh penne, cooked according to the pack instructions. Drain, reserving a little of the cooking water. Return to the pan and stir in 5 tablespoons crème fraîche, adding a little of the cooking water if needed, and crumble over 100 g (3½ oz) blue cheese. Sprinkle over some chopped parsley before serving. **Total cooking time 10 minutes.**

deep-fried haloumi fritters

Serves **4**
Total cooking time **20 minutes**

250 g (8 oz) **plain flour**
1 **egg**, separated
300 ml (½ pint) **ice-cold lager**
125 ml (4 fl oz) **ice-cold water**
vegetable oil, for deep-frying
500 g (1 lb) **haloumi**

To serve
rocket leaves
lemon wedges

Sift the flour into a large bowl and add the egg yolk. Gradually whisk in the lager, then add the measured water and whisk until well combined.

Whisk the egg white in a separate bowl until stiff peaks form. Fold this into the batter.

Fill a deep-fat fryer or a large, deep, heavy-based saucepan two-thirds full with vegetable oil. Heat the oil to 180°C (350°F) or until a cube of bread turns golden in 10–15 seconds.

Cut the haloumi into 1 cm (½ inch) slices, then dip in the batter to coat. Fry the haloumi in batches for 3–4 minutes, or until crisp and golden-brown. Remove with a slotted spoon, season and serve on rocket leaves with wedges of lemon to squeeze over.

For mixed pepper & haloumi skewers, cut 2 deseeded red peppers and 2 deseeded yellow peppers, 2 red onions and 300 g (10 oz) haloumi cheese into bite-sized pieces. Place the vegetables and cheese in a wide bowl. Mix together 2 crushed garlic cloves, 8 tablespoons olive oil, 2 teaspoons dried thyme and the juice and finely grated zest of 1 lemon. Pour over the cheese and vegetables and toss to mix. Thread the vegetables and cheese alternately on to 12 metal skewers. Season and grill under a preheated medium–high grill for 4–5 minutes on each side. Serve immediately. **Total cooking time 10 minutes.**

tagliatelle with dolcelatte & walnuts

Serves **4**

Total cooking time **10 minutes**

350 g (11½ oz) **tagliatelle**

250 ml (8 fl oz) **single cream**

200 g (7 oz) **dolcelatte cheese**, crumbled

100 g (3½ oz) **walnut pieces**, toasted

2 tablespoons shredded **basil leaves**

Cook the pasta in a large saucepan of boiling water for 8–9 minutes, or according to the pack instructions.

Meanwhile, put the single cream in a frying pan with the dolcelatte and place over a medium-low heat. When the cheese is melted, stir in the walnuts.

Drain the pasta and toss in the creamy cheese and walnut sauce.

Serve in warmed bowls, sprinkled with the shredded basil leaves.

For dolcelatte and walnut tortilla pizza, wilt 300 g (10 oz) baby spinach leaves in a saucepan with 1 tablespoon olive oil. Heat 2 tortillas according to the pack instructions. Place the tortillas on baking sheets and spread with a 200 g (7 oz) can chopped tomatoes. Sprinkle with 200 g (7 oz) crumbled dolcelatte and 100 g (3½ oz) toasted walnut pieces. Toast under a preheated hot grill for 3–4 minutes, until bubbling and golden. **Total cooking time 10 minutes.**

roasted roots & feta pearl barley

Serves **4**

Total cooking time **30 minutes**

2 **red onions**, cut into thin
   wedges
16 **carrots**, scrubbed and cut
   into chunks
1 large **raw beetroot**, about
   300 g (10 oz), peeled and
   cut into slim wedges
2–3 tablespoons **olive oil**
1½ teaspoons **cumin seeds**
1½ teaspoons **ground
   coriander**
1½ **vegetable stock cubes**
275 g (9 oz) **pearl barley**
300 g (10 oz) **feta cheese**,
   crumbled
6 tablespoons **fresh coriander
   leaves**

Place all the prepared vegetables in a large roasting
tin, drizzle with the oil and toss to coat. Add the cumin
seeds and ground coriander and toss again. Place
at the top of a preheated oven, 220°C (425°F), Gas
Mark 7, for 20–25 minutes until the vegetables are
tender and lightly charred in places.

Meanwhile, bring a large saucepan of lightly salted
water to the boil, add the stock cubes and pearl barley
and cook for 20 minutes until the grain is tender. Drain,
then toss with the vegetables. Add the crumbled feta
and coriander leaves, toss well and serve.

For carrot, beetroot & feta gratin, heat 3 tablespoons
olive oil in a large frying pan, add 1 large thinly sliced
red onion, 550 g (1 lb 2 oz) peeled and sliced carrots
and 300 g (10 oz) raw beetroot, peeled and cut into
slim wedges, and cook for 8–10 minutes until tender
and cooked through. Add 1½ teaspoons cumin seeds
and ¾ teaspoon ground coriander, then toss and
cook for a further 2 minutes. Divide between 4 small
gratin dishes, then scatter 300 g (10 oz) crumbled
feta cheese over the tops. Cook under a preheated
hot grill for 2–3 minutes until the feta has turned
golden in places. Serve with warm crusty bread. **Total
cooking time 20 minutes.**

creamy walnut & rocket pasta

Serves **4**
Total cooking time **15 minutes**

400 g (13 oz) **orecchiette**
125 g (4 oz) **walnut pieces**
1 **garlic clove**, crushed
4 tablespoons **extra virgin
    olive oil**
75 ml (3 fl oz) **double cream**
50 g (2 oz) grated **Italian-
    style hard cheese**
100 g (3½ oz) **rocket leaves**
salt and **pepper**

Cook the orecchiette in a large saucepan of lightly salted boiling water according to the pack instructions.

Meanwhile, place most of the walnuts, the garlic, oil, cream and grated cheese in a blender or food processor and whizz until smooth. Season to taste.

Drain the pasta, reserving a little of the cooking water, then stir through the walnut sauce, adding a little cooking water if needed. Toss in the rocket leaves and transfer to serving bowls. Top with the reserved walnuts and serve immediately.

For pasta with goats' cheese & walnut sauce,

mix 1 crushed garlic clove with 75 g (3 oz) soft goats' cheese, 75 g (3 oz) cream cheese, 25 g (1 oz) chopped walnuts and a large handful of chopped basil. Season to taste. Cook 500 g (1 lb) fresh pasta in a large pan of lightly salted boiling water according to the pack instructions. Drain, reserving a little of the cooking water. Return to the pan and stir through the sauce, adding a little cooking water if needed. Top with more basil and sprinkle over some more goats' cheese to serve. **Total cooking time 10 minutes.**

desserts

mango and raspberry gratin

Serves **4**
Total cooking time **10 minutes**

125 ml (4 fl oz) **double cream**
150 g (5 oz) **mascarpone cheese**
200 g (7 oz) **ready-made pastry cream** or **custard**
1 **mango**, peeled, pitted and sliced
250 g (8 oz) **raspberries**

Whip the cream until soft peaks form, then carefully stir together with the mascarpone and pastry cream.

Put the mango and raspberries in a small, shallow ovenproof dish and spread the cream mixture on top. Cook very close to a hot grill for 2–3 minutes until lightly browned.

For mango cakes with raspberry sauce, butter 4 individual ramekins or dariole moulds. Mix together 2 tablespoons each softened butter and soft brown sugar and spoon the mixture into the bottom of the ramekins. Add 1 tablespoon chopped mango to each ramekin. Whizz together 100 g (3½ oz) each softened butter, caster sugar and self-raising flour with 2 eggs and 1 teaspoon vanilla extract until a smooth batter forms. Spoon the batter into the ramekins and cook in a preheated oven, 180°C (350°F), Gas Mark 4, for 20–25 minutes until just cooked through. Press 150 g (5 oz) raspberries through a sieve and sift in 1 tablespoon icing sugar to make a sauce. Spoon the sauce over the cakes to serve. **Total cooking time 30 minutes.**

apple, maple & pecan fool

Serves **4**
Total cooking time **10 minutes**

200 g (7 oz) **good-quality apple sauce**
1 **Granny Smith apple**, peeled and grated or finely chopped
200 ml (7 fl oz) **double cream**
250 ml (8 fl oz) **fresh custard**
3 tablespoons **maple syrup**
25 g (1 oz) **pecans**, toasted and chopped
pecan biscuits, to serve

Put the apple sauce and chopped apple in a small saucepan, cook for 5 minutes to soften, then place in metal bowl in the freezer for a few minutes to cool.

Whip the cream until soft peaks form, then stir in the custard. Swirl through the apple purée and maple syrup, then spoon into serving dishes. Top with toasted pecans and serve with pecan biscuits.

For apple & pecan brioches, core and thinly slice 2 Braeburn apples, arrange on a baking sheet and brush over a little melted butter. Cook under a preheated medium grill for 3 minutes on each side until lightly golden. Mix 150 ml (¼ pint) each of milk and cream with 1 egg and 1 teaspoon vanilla extract. Dip 8 slices of brioche in the mixture until well coated. Heat a little butter in a nonstick frying pan and cook the brioche in batches for 2–3 minutes on each side until golden. Arrange the apple slices on top, add spoonfuls of crème fraîche and scatter over chopped pecans. Drizzle with a little maple syrup to serve. **Total cooking time 20 minutes.**

iced berries with white chocolate

Serves **4**
Total cooking time **10 minutes**

175 ml (6 fl oz) **double cream**
175 g (6 oz) **white chocolate**,
  chopped
½ teaspoon **vanilla extract**
500 g (1 lb) **mixed frozen
  berries**

Put the cream in a small saucepan and heat until boiling. Take off the heat and stir in the chocolate and vanilla extract and mix until melted.

Arrange the berries in chilled serving bowls, drizzle over the sauce and serve.

For white chocolate berry mousses, melt 175 g (6 oz) white chocolate in a bowl over a pan of simmering water and leave to cool a little. Beat 200 g (7 oz) cream cheese and mix in 250 ml (8 fl oz) double cream until smooth. Stir in the cooled chocolate. In a separate bowl whisk 3 eggs with 125 g (4 oz) caster sugar until light and fluffy. Fold into the cream cheese mixture, one-third at a time. Place a handful of mixed berries in 4 serving dishes, spoon over some of the cream mixture, followed by some more berries. Keep layering and finish with shavings of white chocolate. **Total cooking time 20 minutes.**

toasted ginger syrup waffles

Serves **4**
Total cooking time **10 minutes**

50 g (2 oz) **butter**
4 tablespoons **double cream**
2 tablespoons **soft dark brown sugar**
15 g (½ oz) **stem ginger**, drained and finely chopped
2 tablespoons **stem ginger syrup**
8 **Belgian-style toasting waffles**
good-quality vanilla ice cream, to serve

Place the butter in a small pan with the cream, sugar, stem ginger and syrup. Warm over a low heat for 5–6 minutes, stirring occasionally, until the butter has melted and the sugar dissolved.

Meanwhile, toast the waffles according to the packet instructions and arrange on serving plates. Top with a scoop of ice cream and serve warm, drizzled with the ginger syrup.

For ginger syrup pain perdu, prepare the ginger syrup as in the recipe above. Meanwhile, place 2 eggs in a large, shallow bowl with 100 g (3½ oz) caster sugar and 250 ml (8 fl oz) milk and whisk until smooth. Dip 4 slices of slightly stale brioche into the mixture, turning to coat both sides. Melt 75 g (3 oz) unsalted butter in a large, nonstick frying pan and cook the brioche over a medium-low heat for 4–5 minutes, turning once, until golden. Arrange on plates and top with a scoop of vanilla ice cream, a dusting of icing sugar and a drizzle of the ginger syrup. **Total cooking time 20 minutes.**

baked honeyed figs & raspberries

Serves **4**
Total cooking time **20 minutes**

8 **figs**, quartered
150 g (5 oz) **raspberries**
4 tablespoons **clear honey**
finely grated rind of 1 medium
 orange
coconut ice cream, to serve

Cut 4 large squares of foil. Divide the figs and raspberries between the pieces of foil, drizzle over the honey and sprinkle with the orange rind.

Bring the edges of the foil up to the centre and twist to form parcels. Place on a large baking sheet and bake in a preheated oven, 200°C (400°F), Gas Mark 6, for 15 minutes.

Open the parcels and serve the fruit and juices with spoonfuls of coconut ice cream.

For fig, raspberry & honey yogurt pots, crumble 8 ginger biscuits and spoon into 4 glasses. Divide 4 chopped figs and 150 g (5 oz) raspberries between the glasses and drizzle each with honey. Spoon 3 tablespoons coconut yogurt over each and serve each topped with a raspberry. **Total cooking time 10 minutes.**

orange & strawberry salad

Serves **4**
Total cooking time **10 minutes**

60 g (2¼ oz) **caster sugar**
100 ml (3½ fl oz) **water**
1 tablespoon thinly sliced
  basil leaves
150 g (5 oz) **strawberries**,
  hulled and halved
4 **oranges**

Put the sugar and measured water in a saucepan and bring to the boil. Simmer for 2–3 minutes, then let it cool briefly before adding the basil.

Place the strawberries in a bowl. Peel and segment 4 oranges over the bowl to catch the juice. Add the orange segments to the strawberries.

Pour in the sugar syrup and serve.

For caramelized oranges, peel 4 oranges, then slice them thinly. Place in a shallow serving dish and pour over 1 tablespoon orange liqueur. Place 115 g (3¾ oz) granulated sugar, 1 cinnamon stick and 150 ml (¼ pint) water in a saucepan. Heat, stirring, until the sugar has dissolved. Continue to simmer until the sugar starts to caramelize and turns a rich caramel colour. Pour the syrup over the oranges. Decorate with 25 g (1 oz) toasted pine nuts and 1 tablespoon chopped mint leaves. **Total cooking time 20 minutes.**

lemon puddings

Serves **4**
Total cooking time **30 minutes**

50 g (2 oz) **butter**
125 g (4 oz) **caster sugar**
2 **eggs**, separated
50 g (2 oz) **plain flour**
150 ml (¼ pint) **milk**
150 ml (¼pint) **single cream**
finely grated rind of 1 **lemon**
 and juice of ½ lemon
icing sugar, to serve

Put the butter and sugar in a bowl and beat with a hand-held electric whisk until pale and creamy. Add the egg yolks and mix in well, then stir in the flour. Gradually whisk in the milk and cream, followed by the lemon rind and juice.

Whisk the egg whites until stiff peaks form. Stir one-third of the whites into the batter. Then carefully fold in the remainder, half at a time. Spoon the mixture into 4 individual ramekins and bake in a preheated oven, 180°C (350°F), Gas Mark 4, for 15 minutes or until golden. Dust with icing sugar to serve.

For lemon mousse, using a hand-held electric whisk, mix together 300 ml (½ pint) double cream, 75 g (3 oz) caster sugar and the finely grated rind of 1 lemon. Stir in 1 tablespoon lemon juice or to taste and whisk until smooth. Whisk 2 egg whites until stiff peaks form. Stir a spoonful of the mixture into the whipped cream, then carefully fold in the remainder, half at a time. Spoon into serving bowls and grate over some more lemon rind to serve. **Total cooking time 20 minutes.**

warm chocolate cherry tarts

Serves **4**

Total cooking time **20 minutes**

200 g (7 oz) **plain dark chocolate**, broken into pieces

3 tablespoons **double cream**

1 tablespoon **brandy**

2 **eggs** and 1 **egg yolk**

50 g (2 oz) **caster sugar**

50 g (2 oz) **undyed glacé cherries**, halved

4 **ready-made individual pastry cases**

Put the chocolate, cream and brandy in a small bowl. Set it over a saucepan of gently simmering water, so the bottom of the bowl is not touching the water, and heat for a couple of minutes until the chocolate is melted. Leave to cool a little.

Whisk together the eggs, egg yolk and sugar with a hand-held electric whisk until pale and creamy. Carefully stir the chocolate mixture into the eggs. Arrange the cherries in the pastry cases, pour over the chocolate mixture and bake in a preheated oven, 190°C (375°F), Gas Mark 5, for 12 minutes or until just set.

For cherries with chocolate dipping sauce, heat 200 ml (7 fl oz) double cream in a pan until boiling. Put 200 g (7 oz) chopped plain dark chocolate in a bowl. Pour the cream over and stir until smooth. Add a splash of brandy or kirsch, if liked. Place in a warm serving bowl and serve with fresh cherries for dunking. **Total cooking time 10 minutes.**

blueberry & banana french toast

Serves **4**

Total cooking time **20 minutes**

2 **eggs**

4 tablespoons **milk**

4 teaspoons **caster sugar**

4 slices of **crusty white bread**

50 g (2 oz) **butter**

50 g (2 oz) **blueberries**

2 **bananas**, sliced

To serve

ice cream

maple syrup

Beat together the eggs, milk and 2 teaspoons of the caster sugar in a jug. Pour into a shallow dish and dip both sides of the bread slices into the egg mixture.

Heat the butter in a large frying pan, add the bread (you might need to cook 1 slice at a time) and cook for 2 minutes on each side until crisp and golden. Sprinkle over the remaining sugar.

Cut the French toasts in half diagonally and scatter with the blueberries and banana slices. Serve with ice cream and a drizzle of maple syrup.

For blueberry pancakes with banana, place 75 g (3 oz) self-raising flour, 1 tablespoon caster sugar, 1 egg and 75 ml (3 fl oz) milk in a food processor or blender and blitz together to make a smooth, thick batter. Stir in 25 g (1 oz) blueberries. Heat 1 tablespoon sunflower oil in a large frying pan, add 2 large spoonfuls of the batter and cook for 1–2 minutes on each side until golden. Repeat with the remaining batter to make another 2 pancakes. Serve warm with sliced banana and a drizzle of honey. **Total cooking time 10 minutes.**

sambuca watermelon & pineapple

Serves **4**

Total cooking time **10 minutes**

½ **small watermelon**

1 **small pineapple**

4 shots of **Sambuca**

2 tablespoons **toasted flaked almonds**

4 scoops of **vanilla ice cream, to serve**

Peel the watermelon and pineapple and cut into 1 cm (½ inch) thick slices.

Stack the slices on top of each other on 4 serving plates, alternating the fruits.

Pour 1 shot of the Sambuca over each, sprinkle with the flaked almonds and serve with a scoop of vanilla ice cream.

For pineapple fritters, sift 200 g (7 oz) plain flour into a bowl, then whisk in 125 ml (4 fl oz) warm water, 100 ml (3½ oz) beer, ½ tablespoon vegetable oil and ½ tablespoon marsala to make a batter. Cut 1 large cored and peeled pineapple into thick slices. Pour sunflower oil into a deep-fat fryer or large saucepan and heat to 180–190°C (350–375°F), or until a cube of bread dropped into the oil browns in 30 seconds. Whisk 2 egg whites into the batter and then dip in the pineapple slices, shaking off any excess. Working in batches if necessary, carefully drop into the hot oil. Deep-fry for 3–4 minutes, until golden all over. Remove with a slotted spoon and drain on kitchen paper. Serve scattered with torn mint leaves and dusted with caster sugar. **Total cooking time 30 minutes.**

cherry & vanilla brûlée

Serves **4**
Total cooking time **10 minutes**

300 g (10 oz) **ripe cherries**,
 stoned and roughly chopped
12 tablespoons **caster sugar**
50 g (2 oz) **glacé cherries**,
 roughly chopped
4 tablespoons **kirsch or
 cherry liqueur**
400 ml (14 fl oz) **vanilla
 yogurt**

Mix the fresh cherries in a bowl with the half the sugar, the chopped glacé cherries and kirsch.

Spoon the cherry mixture into 4 glass ramekins and top with the yogurt.

Sprinkle the remaining caster sugar over the yogurt and use a blow-torch (or place the ramekins under a preheated hot grill for 2–3 minutes) to caramelize the tops. Serve immediately.

For cherry & raspberry brûlée, place a mixture of 300 g (10 oz) stoned cherries and 300 g (10 oz) raspberries in a shallow ovenproof dish. Spoon over 400 ml (14 fl oz) fresh ready-made custard and sprinkle over 4 tablespoons caster sugar. Cook under a preheated medium-high grill for 4–5 minutes or until lightly browned and bubbling. Serve immediately. **Total cooking time 10 minutes.**

index

234

acknowledgements

Commissioning editor: Eleanor Maxfield
Senior editor: Leanne Bryan
Design manager: Jaz Bahra
Designer: Tracy Killick
Picture library manager: Jen Veall
Production controller: Sarah Kramer

Octopus Publishing Group Stephen Conroy 10–11, 23, 31, 53, 88–89, 101, 129, 136–137, 159, 193; Will Heap 1, 2–3, 4–5, 6, 7, 8, 9 left, 25, 29, 33, 35, 39, 41, 43, 57, 61, 67, 69, 79, 95, 97, 103, 113, 119, 125, 133, 139, 141, 143, 145, 147, 149, 153, 155, 157, 165, 167, 169, 171, 172–173, 175, 177, 179, 185, 187, 189, 191, 195, 197, 199, 201, 203, 209, 213, 215, 217, 219, 225, 227, 233; Lis Parsons 9 right, 15, 17, 19, 21, 27, 37, 59, 65, 73, 75, 77, 83, 85, 91, 99, 105, 107, 121, 123, 127, 131, 151, 181, 183, 207, 221, 223, 229, 231; William Reavell 13, 47, 49, 81, 109, 117, 135, 161, 163; William Shaw 45, 51, 63, 71, 87, 93, 111, 115, 205, 210–211; Ian Wallace 54–55.